Growing Up South
of the Mason-Dixon Line

Growing Up South of the Mason-Dixon Line

13 Stories

MICHAEL BRASWELL
and
ANTHONY CAVENDER

With
RALPH BLAND
and
DONALD BALL

RESOURCE *Publications* · Eugene, Oregon

Growing Up South of the Mason-Dixon Line
13 Stories

Resource Publications
An Imprint of Wipf and Stock Publishers
199 W. 8th Ave., Suite 3
Eugene, OR 97401

www.wipfandstock.com

PAPERBACK ISBN: 978-1-7252-5799-3
HARDCOVER ISBN: 978-1-7252-5800-6
EBOOK ISBN: 978-1-7252-5801-3

Manufactured in the U.S.A.   01/08/20

Contents

Acknowledgments

WE WANT TO THANK CINDY DAVIS, SUSAN BRASWELL, AND EMILY Callihan for their help with our manuscript.

"Invisible Boy" was previously published in *Morality Stories* and "Hold the line" was previously published in *Remembering Peleliu*. "Second Street" was previously published in *Stray Dogs*.

Some of the stories in this collection are composites of several memories and events the authors experienced. Names of the persons in the stories have been changed.

I

Second Street

Michael Braswell

"It's a damn hot day," Big M exclaimed while straddling his three speed Schwinn in the alleyway between First and Second Street.

"Damn hot," repeated Little M, his nine-year-old brother, standing beside him. Little M never really talked much until Big M spoke. Then he simply repeated in some form or fashion whatever this older brother said. Nobody really knew how the two brothers got to be known as Big M and Little M. The older brother was eleven, short and stocky while his younger sibling was tall and skinny. Their given names were Marvin and Theodore, respectively. Their mother called them Marty and Ted while their father succumbed to neighborhood tradition and referred to them as Big M. and Little M except when he was mad.

Then he simply bellowed their gender, "Boy."

The two brothers lived on Second Street, one of four streets that made up Magnolia Estates in the small South Georgia town of Mulberry. It was a nice enough neighborhood although the six-room, shingle-sided tract houses could hardly be called estates and no one ever remembered seeing a magnolia tree. Rumor had it that Hubert Holbrook, the developer, did cut down two magnolia trees that interfered with some road grading when he first started developing the neighborhood.

Magnolia Estates was referred to by real estate brokers as a nice, middle class neighborhood. It was true that most families who lived there thought of themselves as middle class. In reality, except for First Street, everybody else was on the low side of middle class. First Street was different. It faced the paved two-lane highway that connected Mulberry with Newberry, twenty miles away. The people who lived on First Street were honest-to-goodness middle class although they thought of themselves as upper-middle class. Their houses were made of brick or wood siding and had garages and brick barbecue pits. Two families on First Street even had above-ground swimming pools. Hot summer days found those pools full of yelling, splashing First Street children, while their mothers sat in folding chairs or reclined on beach towels trying to get the beginning of a tan before their annual three-day, Panama City beach vacations. Second through Fourth Street children were not invited. They had to settle for playing with a water hose, running through their Mom's sprinkler system, or taking their chances in a nearby creek or fishing pond. Maybe that's why on a humid night in mid-July, Big M and Jimmy Simpkins, his best friend who lived on Third Street, punched a dozen or more holes through each of the pool's sidewalls while little M stood watch in the alleyway.

Big M, Little M, and Jimmy Simpkins were inseparable whenever they weren't in school. There were three boys like all other nine to eleven-year-olds experiencing the long hot, slow summers of South Georgia. Whether sneaking around in someone's yard when the occupants weren't home or exploring the oak and yellow pine forests that surrounded them, each day was a new adventure. Had it not been for two inventions these three young boys and countless others like them would have perhaps, spent their summer days more productively.

The BB gun and the bicycle transformed young boys from the artistry of crayons and coloring books to marauding bandits, on the move and ready for action. With their three-speed Schwinns and Daisy rapid-fire, lever-action BB guns, Big M, Little M, and Jimmy Simpkins defended their turf ruthlessly, especially when it came to any hapless kids who ventured from First Street. The streets were for cars and adults, but the alleyways were their domain, a kind of no-man's land fraught with danger and surprise attacks.

Leaning on his bicycle's handle-bars, Big M turned to his little brother and whispered, "I think I see Billy Ray Wilson. I bet he's gonna try and catch some minnows. Ride over to Jimmy's and the two of you meet me at the creek."

Little M nodded his assent with the seriousness of a special agent carrying out a dangerous assignment. He left in a cloud of dust, his skinny legs pedaling as fast as they could toward Jimmy's house.

Big M carefully loaded the BB's into his Daisy with delicate precision. His lips curled into a smile as he thought about his prey, Billy Ray Wilson, and the fun he and his compadres were going to have. Mr. big-shot, Billy Ray Wilson, was about to learn a thing or two. His fancy, chrome-fendered bicycle with the genuine leather saddle bags wouldn't do him any good when Big M and the boys got hold of him. It didn't matter if he and his chiropractor father, mother, and little sister lived in the biggest house on first street or not. When he used the alley or "thunder road" as Jimmy liked to call it, he was dead meat.

Big M wasn't really a bad kid. His parents' friends referred to him as a "spirited child." Adults who weren't acquainted with his parents called him a "little devil" or worse. In today's world a psychologist would probably describe him as an Attention Deficit-Hyperactive child. In the sixties there wasn't any Ritalin or related drugs, only keen switches at the hand of his mother to settle him down or a foot in his behind from his father to put the fear of the Lord into him. Big M once mentioned to his best friend Jimmy that he did not know the Lord well enough to be afraid of him, but he sure was afraid of his Daddy.

A bicycle, a BB gun and a couple of followers brought out the predatory instincts Big M possessed. He liked dangerous situations. The only thing he liked better than walking on the edge of danger himself was instilling fear and terror in others. Whatever the case, on that day, things didn't look good for Billy Ray Wilson. Big M's eyes narrowed as he chuckled to himself, peddling his bicycle ever faster toward the creek.

Billy Ray was bending over the creek, carefully working his minnow net through its waters when he heard the boys come up behind him. Big M stood in the middle of the path that led to the creek, flanked on both sides by Little M and Jimmy. Holding his Daisy air rifle in his left hand and wearing a pair of red-frame, superman sunglasses, Big M, who always had a flare for the dramatic, was more than a little cocky. Jimmy also looked confident, but not Little M. He shifted his weight from one foot to the other and held his BB gun as though he was afraid it might go off.

"Billy Boy, what do you think you're doing, riding down our alley and messing in our creek," Big M said in his most menacing voice.

"Yeah, who gave you permission, Silly Billy," chimed in Jimmy Simpkins.

"Yeah, Billy Boy," echoed Little M, who seemed to be gaining more confidence by the moment.

Billy Ray Wilson stumbled backwards, knocking over his minnow bucket. Beads of sweat began to break out on his forehead.

"I ain't doing nothing but trying to get me some minnows. This here's public property." Conjuring up all the false courage he could muster, Billy Ray continued, "It's a free country. My daddy said I could ride in the alley anytime I wanted to."

Big M inched towards Billy Ray, holding his air rifle with both hands. "Is that so, Billy boy? Your daddy's full of cow manure. He ain't even a real doctor."

"He is so a real doctor!" Billy Ray retorted, his red face raining sweat.

Almost in unison, Little M and Jimmy shouted at Billy Ray, "You're full of cow manure. Big M, let's make him eat boogers like we did last time!"

"Maybe later, but not just yet." Big M cocked his lever-action rapid-fire Daisy. "First, we need to teach Billy Boy a lesson for trespassing on our private property. "

Jimmy and Little M responded with a resounding "Yeah, that's right."

If Billy Ray Wilson had been raised differently and had not lived such a sheltered life, he would have realized that at twelve going on thirteen years of age, he was twice as big as any of the three boys confronting him. He could more than hold his own in a fight with any of them, but he didn't see himself that way. Inside he felt small and scared and wished he were home eating a Popsicle. All he could offer in his defense was a desperate, empty threat.

"I'll tell my daddy if you don't leave me alone."

As if on cue, Big M, Little M, and Jimmy Simpkins began laughing. Aiming his air rifle at Billy Ray's feet, Big M fired off a round and shouted, "Dance Billy Boy dance." And Billy Ray tried to do just that, but he really didn't know how. A second and third shot from Big M's Daisy kicked up little puffs of sand. The fourth shot hit Billy Ray in the left foot, stinging him through his black and white Converse tennis shoes. Then he wet his pants and began to cry. More laughter and taunts of "Cry Baby" erupted from his three tormentors.

Suddenly, Billy Ray surprised everyone by jumping into the waist-deep creek where water moccasins had been spotted on more than one occasion and a mythical alligator was rumored to have eaten Arthur Johansen's poodle. He half-waded and dog paddled to the other side. Soaking wet, Billy Ray sloshed furiously through the blackberry bushes and brambles as fast as he could, running through the woods toward the safety of home.

"Let's catch him when he cuts through old Lady Fowler's back yard," shouted Big M as the three BB gun-toting marauders scrambled for their Schwinns.

Billy Ray ran hard and breathed harder, his water-logged sneakers squished their way toward First Street, while the predators pursued him in a cloud of summer dust. All four boys were sweating profusely—one from fear and the others from the thrill of the hunt.

Everything in life depends on one's perspective. Leona Fowler and her friend Myrtle observed the chase on their way to the Shoe Mart's semi-annual sale in Newberry. The two women shook their heads with a certain disdain as they drove by in Myrtle's Ford Fairlane.

Myrtle pursed her lips, "Leona, would you look at that? Those Jones boys and the Simpkins' son are chasing another boy."

Leona Fowler, a widow of ten years, had viewed similar incidents from her kitchen window and had dutifully reported each one in detail to her friends through extended party-line, telephone conversations.

With a disapproving tone, she replied "Doesn't surprise me a bit. Those second street hellions are always up to no good. I should know. They've trampled and torn up my flower beds more than once. The boy they're after is Billy Ray Wilson. His father is a professional man."

To Leona and Myrtle, the event was a minor intrusion into their morning shopping spree, nothing more than a childish prank. To Big M, Little M, Jimmy and Billy Ray it was an epic struggle. As far as Billy Ray Wilson was concerned, he was literally running for his life. He remembered the booger-eating incident all too well, not to mention the BB gun induced dancing that comprised his most recent humiliation.

Billy Ray was a settler who had foolishly ventured too far from the safety of the fort and had been caught in a surprise attack with no means of defense. As he pushed his body to its physical limits, he promised himself that next time, he would pay more attention to his surroundings—if there was a next time.

To someone like Leona Fowler, Big M, Little M, and Jimmy were "hellions." To Billy Ray, they were worse than that; they were more like the devil incarnate. The three boys, however, saw themselves as heroes, protecting their homesteads from the carpet-bagging likes of Billy Ray Wilson and other First Street land barons.

Billy Ray almost made it, but not quite. Jimmy, the fastest of the three, cut off his escape route while Big M and Little M surrounded him. Billy Ray, panting from the heat of a blistering hot Georgia sun, found refuge in Leona Fowler's metal utility building. He hunkered down in a back corner of the shed. The late Mr. Fowler's yard tiller and self-propelled lawn mower was all that stood between him and Armageddon. All he could do was clutch a broken-handled yard rake and shout over and over, "You better leave me alone!"

Meanwhile, Big M showed Little M and Jimmy how to aim their air rifles at an angle so the BB's would ricochet off the walls and ceiling of the metal building. When one of the stinging projectiles found its mark, a yelp of pain from Billy Ray was their reward for persistence. After inflicting a barrage of BB gunfire, the three boys eventually became bored. Big M concocted a variation of their torturous game. Several times they rode down the alley, pretending to leave only to circle back and hide behind a nearby hedgerow. As soon as Billy Ray tried to emerge from the utility building, he would be met by a hailstorm of BB's from his well-concealed attackers, sending him back in full retreat to the rear of the building. Each time they pretended to leave he would wait longer before trying to make his get-away. Each time he was fooled and sent scurrying back into the building. The torment continued for almost two hours with no relief in sight when a miracle happened. Big M and Little M heard Miss Emma ring the dinner bell.

Even families on the back side of middle class could afford maids in the 1950s. Low wages and no benefits aside, even bad jobs were scarce for black women. The dinner bell rang a second and a third time. Big M and Little M looked at each other and smacked their lips. That sound could mean only one thing—chicken pot pies and maybe a little left-over peach cobbler for dessert. Chicken pot pies, four for a dollar at the local Winn-Dixie, were the hardtack and field rations of the fighting boys of Second Street.

Big M left Jimmy on sentry duty with strict orders: "Keep Billy Ray cornered until we return from lunch. Fire a few rounds ever so often to keep him trapped." No excuses would be accepted. Jimmy's reward for following orders would be that he would escape Big M's wrath and would be treated to some of Miss Emma's peach cobbler after they had completed their mission.

As always, Miss Emma's pot pies were superb. However, the peach cobbler was not to be. It had been requisitioned by the boys' father as dessert for his and their mother's evening meal. Big M and Little M would have to settle for a graham cracker to go with the last of their milk.

Wiping the cracker crumbs from his Batman tee shirt, Big M was none too happy about missing out on the peach cobbler. And as far as he was concerned, in a few minutes, Billy Ray Wilson was going to pay the price for that disappointment.

Full of chicken pie, graham crackers, and milk, Big M and Little M felt refreshed and re-energized. Mounting their trusty Schwinns, they were ready to return to battle. Little M carefully wrapped two graham crackers in a paper napkin and stuffed them in his tee-shirt. It wasn't the peach cobbler he had promised Jimmy, but it was better than nothing.

As Big M and Little M turned the corner toward Old Lady Fowler's yard, it was eerily silent. There were no sounds of BBs ricocheting off metal walls or taunts, or screams of pain—only a couple of blue jays squawking and a dog barking in the distance.

"I don't like the sound of this," Big M grumbled, cocking his Daisy, " I don't like it one bit!"

"Where's Jimmy?" Little M whispered as he and his older brother surveyed their most recent battlefield, later referred to in various historical renditions as "Old Lady Fowler's building" or just the "Fight at Fowler's Place."

Their search first led them to the building itself, where there was no sign of Billy Ray or Jimmy. Their calls for Jimmy initially went unanswered. They found him sprawled on the ground, moaning and holding his bruised head, a casualty of a desperate counter attack.

Apparently Billy Ray Wilson had finally come to his senses. As confused and frightened as he was, he came to the conclusion that his chances, unarmed or not, were better against one than against three. His body, pumped up on adrenaline was more than ready for a dash to freedom. He was still afraid, but he sensed intuitively that his best chance for survival was to make his move.

At first he tried negotiating.

"Hey Jimmy, why don't you let me go?"

"No way," came the terse reply, followed by several quick rounds from Jimmy's air rifle.

The clock was ticking. It wouldn't be long before Big M and Little M returned and the torture resumed.

"Hey Jimmy, I'll give you my original Mickey Mantle baseball card if you'll let me go."

Billy Ray had upped his ante. He had gotten Jimmy's attention. The only thing Jimmy Simpkins liked as much as riding and shooting was playing baseball and collecting baseball cards.

Jimmy didn't answer right away. He was thinking the proposition over. Bribing one's guard to escape punishment is as old as history. Of course, Billy Ray Wilson had no intention of giving Jimmy his Topps Mickey Mantle card, but Jimmy didn't know that. He was considering whether or not such a rare treasure was worth Big M's wrath. Billy Ray was lying to Jimmy and Jimmy was wondering if he could tell a convincing lie to Big M. Absorbed with several possible scenarios, Jimmy laid his BB gun on the ground and began to rub his chin with his right hand, a nervous habit that signaled the rare occasion when he was trying to use his mind.

The distraction was enough.

When Billy Ray Wilson saw Jimmy drop his Daisy, every cell in his large body came alive in a spurt of self-preservation. From some former gene pool deep inside him emerged a blood-curdling rebel yell as he charged his tormentor. Eyes wide open with surprise, Jimmy reached for his Daisy and thinking better of it turned to run. Too late. Billy Ray lunged at him, half on purpose and half because he tripped over his size eleven tennis shoes. Whatever his intention was, the end result was that Billy Ray did a full belly-flop on Jimmy Simpkins. When they hit the ground, you could hear the air go out of Jimmy like a punctured birthday party balloon. Jimmy Simpkins lay in a crumpled heap on the ground, his right leg trembling uncontrollably. He wanted to cry, but first he had to get his breath. Realizing his advantage, Billy Ray picked up the air rifle. Holding the barrel with both hands, he pretended he was chopping wood on Jimmy's head. While Jimmy clutched his head and wailed in pain, Billy Ray took one last arching swing against a yellow pine, breaking the Daisy in two pieces.

Yelling "Home Run," Billy Ray Wilson ran victoriously toward the safety of First Street. His final action only increased Jimmy's agony, "You broke my gun, you broke my gun," he groaned between sobs.

Of course, the story Jimmy Simpkins told Big M when he arrived ten minutes later was slightly different. There was no mention of the Mickey Mantle baseball card or of Jimmy's inclination to abandon his post when Billy Ray charged him. As memory served him best, he stood his ground and after throwing several devastating punches was finally overwhelmed by Billy Ray's superior size. As best he could tell, he must have gotten knocked unconscious when Billy Ray hit him over the head with his air rifle.

To be fair, when Billy discussed the day's events with his chiropractor father, his memory proved to be selective as well. Forgotten were the dancing and wet pants or the crying and begging for mercy, and most certainly the attempted bribe. Instead, there was one against three—good versus evil. It was high noon and Billy Ray was Gary Cooper. All he had were his fists against three punks with air rifles. Sure he got hit with several BB shots as his mother listened in horror. But then, no pain, no gain. He knew somehow he had to get to the ringleader of the Second Street terrorists. It wasn't Jimmy Simpkins that he disarmed and beat over the head with the assailant's own weapon. No, it was Big M himself.

"Big M!" his little sister exclaimed in awe.

Of course, it was Big M. After that, the other two fled for their lives.

As evening drew near, Big M, Little M and Jimmy Simpkins said their goodbyes before turning their bicycles homeward.

"Billy Ray Wilson better watch out," Big M imparted to his fellow marauders, "Tomorrow will be payback time."

Of course, every day was payback time for somebody as far as Big M was concerned. And Billy Ray said pretty much the same thing as he finished his version of the day's battle. Rising from the dinner table with his father giving him a "that's my boy" smile, his mother still looking horrified, and his little sister beaming with a pride that could only come from having a big brother who had whipped the notorious Big M, Billy Ray's final words were: "All I can say is Big M and his two sidekicks better watch out if they cross my path again."

It should be noted that although both boys said pretty much the same thing, there was a certain distinction regarding the meaning of their comments.

Big M meant what he said and Billy Ray Wilson did not.

2

The Bible Belt

MICHAEL BRASWELL

"BOY, COME HERE" SIGNALED A FOUR ALARM CALL TO JUSTICE. Daddy was home.

Like Santa Claus, Momma had been keeping a list and checking it twice, but there was no seeing who had been naughty or nice. If you were on the list, it meant two things. You had been subjected to thinly veiled threats and reminders throughout the day about what was to come from your Mother, who was no less than a Samurai Master when it came to psychological intimidation. Of course, the four boys who comprised the Smith household already knew what was to come. They were experienced veterans of the "Bible Belt" and as psychological prisoners of war, the rules of the Geneva Convention didn't apply.

All roads led to the First Baptist Church on Sunday. Sunday School, the morning service, Baptist Training Union, and the evening service wrapped the day up. The only reward as far as the Smith boys were concerned was the quick ride home in their 1956 two-tone burgundy and white Chevrolet station wagon so their father, C.L., could whip up mustard-laden pastrami sandwiches with pickles, chips and sweet tea for supper. The family would sit in their den munching and sipping as they waited with bated breath for the next episode of Bonanza in all its brilliant Technicolor glory. Before that glorious end to the day, Sunday's rituals had to be honored.

Their father sounded his own version of reveille on Sunday mornings, signaling to one and all that it was time to get ready for church. White shirts, clip-on ties, pressed pants and polished shoes had to pass inspection before breakfast. Oh yes, and combed hair. Boot-camp style haircuts required no more than a quick run-through with the Butch Wax tube to make sure the hair in front stood at attention. The older brothers were treated by C.L. to a handful of Vitalis, the hair care product of choice preferred by their father. The high alcohol content was potent enough to make the younger boys swoon as they staggered to breakfast. Ralph, who later as an adult, worked in the local prison, found out that Vitalis was a beverage of choice for inmates who could afford it.

C.L. Smith loved to sing. While he was still working on the farm with his Mother and brothers as share croppers he formed a gospel quartet with one of his brothers and two other friends. Now, years later he still liked to belt out an old hymn or gospel tune in the church choir or in concert with the radio while he was getting dressed for church. "Just a little talk with Jesus" was one of his favorites.

Sunday church was, indeed, a momentous occasion in the Smith household. Rows of pews in three sections, ushers marching down the aisle with military precision to take up the offering just before the special music and main event, the sermon, began. Who could forget the vocal solos of Priscilla Abelour? Close to six foot in stature and the heft to go with it, her solos combined singing with the dramatic flair of a one-act play. Just at the right moment she would fling her arms wide and look to the heavens as her powerful voice reached a concluding crescendo. Ralph's buddy, Jerome, was once forced to watch an Opera with his Aunt Matilda from Atlanta. He claimed the only thing Priscilla Abelour was missing when she sang was one of those Viking helmets like the women wore on stage in the big city.

Then came the preaching. Reverend Devane was a bit long-winded, especially when it came Invitation time. Ten stanzas of "Just As I Am" were not unusual as he implored the congregation to make a profession of faith or rededicate themselves to a closer walk with Jesus. If the Invitation lasted too long, the Smith boys were prone to get restless. On such occasions, their Mother employed a technique she had perfected for just such a circumstance—the "corkscrew." First, she would offer her rambunctious child a warning look. If that didn't work, she looked straight ahead while she activated a stealth move. Using only her thumb and index finger, she located the offender's soft tissue on the side just above his waist. A pinch and clockwise turn was all it took to settle him down. The trick was to inflict enough pain to render him helpless, but not so much as to elicit a holler of pain.

Sometimes extended invitations worked their magic like the time Bevo Watkins walked down the aisle at the last minute, sobbing with regret and asking God's and his father's forgiveness for his wayward life. Women were crying and men were shouting "Amen." Even the Smith brothers paid rapt attention to the miracle of restoration that was happening before their very eyes.

There was the Sunday before Christmas when Eddie Cox, himself a lay minister, was smoking Camel cigarettes outside with a group of fellow Deacons. He asked his wife if she had seen their seven-year-old son, Eddie, Jr. Thelma's glance said it all. Her husband, not her, was responsible for keeping tabs on their high-spirited boy. She looked in the vestibule and around the side of the building where children often played. No sign of Eddie. Then she heard an unfamiliar sound coming from the Sanctuary. She felt the hair stand up on her neck as she opened the door. The church was about half full. The organist hadn't arrived nor had the choir taken their place in the choir loft. To her utter horror, little Eddie was standing next to the pulpit, microphone in hand, pointing a toy cowboy pistol he had received in his Sunday School gift exchange and pretending to shoot at members of the congregation. Thelma knew she had to act fast. She positioned herself behind the last row of the middle section and strained to get her son's attention. Finally, Eddie caught wind of his mother's ominous glare. Thelma emphatically motioned for her son to come to her. Perhaps, little Ed felt empowered because he was onstage. Whatever the reason, instead of running to his mother, he mimicked her motion with one of his own. The result was that the church members who had been watching Eddie turned around to see who the boy was waving at. No doubt, things didn't go well for Eddie, Sr. or Jr. after the service was over.

Before church started, folks mingled and made small talk. When church ended, those same members hustled their children to Fords, Chevys and Chryslers in an effort to beat the others to "The Gold Leaf Restaurant" for the Sunday lunch special. Of course, the Methodists always got there first. They didn't extend the Invitation. They were smart in that way. People stood in line outside waiting for an available table in order to enjoy a cup of chicken and rice soup, a slice of turkey and a scoop of dressing along with a spoonful of green beans. The coup de grace was a small bowl of banana pudding. Bertrand and Agnes Fletcher didn't order the common fare of working families with children. Instead, they ordered grilled steaks brought out on sizzling platters with hot baked potatoes slathered with butter and sour cream. No banana pudding for them when it came to desert. Generous slices of hot apple pie crowned by a scoop of vanilla ice cream was their reward for cleaning their plate. Maybe it was because Bertrand worked at the bank or because they had no children. Whatever the reason, the Fletchers ate their bounty with a subtle smugness which seemed to ward off the sharp glances and asides thrown their way by the turkey and dressing crowd.

One might assume that Sundays being a day of rest Biblically speaking, C.L.'s belt would rest on the belt rack as well. Such was not the case. In fact, the worst whipping Ralph, the oldest boy, ever received was on a memorable Sunday after the morning service. Ralph's mother had relented and given her twelve-year-old eldest son permission to sit with Leroy Davis. Since the Smiths always sat in the right section, Ralph and Leroy chose to sit in the left section counting on a full middle section to provide them cover from the prying eyes of their parents. They had a grand time sliding back and forth on their nearly empty pew, throwing spitballs crafted from the Sunday morning bulletin and writing in the hymnal. It wasn't until the choir was about to sing the Invitation hymn that Ralph began to get the feeling that all wasn't right in his universe. Looking up at the choir loft he found none other than his father staring back at him with dead eyes. There was no lunch time meal at the Gold Leaf that day. It was straight home for whipping time. It was a whipping Ralph would always remember. It was the one time his mother didn't egg his father on, but rather intervened with "C.L. you need to stop. You might leave marks."

Of course, Ralph wasn't alone when it came to discipline time. His other brothers, Mason, Marvin and Alex all heard their father's beck and call, "Come here, boy" from time to time. C.L. was versatile when it came to administering justice. A belt here, a leaf rake there, and even a wingtip lace-up shoe served more than one purpose. In those days, a man's size ten wingtip was to shoes what a Sherman tank was to a military assault. One night when Marvin came home drunk from a night on the town, C.L. pinned him in the bathtub and armed with nothing more than one of his reliable wingtips, hammered him into submission. In today's world, a heavy-duty wingtip might well qualify for registration as a potentially lethal weapon.

Their father's prized implement for both holding up his trousers and distributing justice was his Buxton belt. As one brother put it, "If you heard the tinkle of the belt buckle, it was too late to run." C.L. was Indiana Jones before Indiana Jones was cool. Who needed a whip when a Buxton belt was available? His effective range of attack was 180 degrees although he was known on occasion to place a well-timed pop behind his head. When one of the brothers tried to dance out of reach of the lash, C.L. would deploy what came to be referred to as "the guillotine." Standing upright, he would position their head between his legs. It was "bottoms up" time. Unable to move but a few inches to the left or right, the Buxton easily found its target.

In the Smith household, the Buxton belt was the Bible belt. The child was not spoiled nor the rod spared. Of course, most of the time the Smith brothers were hardly innocent victims. They were a rambunctious lot like many of their neighborhood allies, always looking for creative ways to get into trouble. In those days, parents felt it was their duty to nip trouble in the bud before the devil took hold.

Years later, well into adulthood, the Smith clan would gather together for the holidays. After an evening meal of Christmas leftovers all would gather around the fireplace and reminisce about the past. The Smith brothers would inevitably begin to revel in tales about their growing up days, often exaggerating about the utility and function of the Bible belt. Everyone would laugh until their sides hurt. As the tales progressed, the laughter would increase except for their father. He would sit among them, chuckling and smiling from time to time, drumming his fingers on the arm of his recliner.

3

Fort Apache

MICHAEL BRASWELL

"INCOMING!" REX SHOUTED AS A DIRT CLOD THE SIZE OF A BASE-ball crashed through the living room window sending glass shards in every direction.

Picking up his coonskin cap and dusting it off, he placed it back on his head and picked up his rifle.

"Looks like the fourth street boys are trying to advance from our rear," Joey shouted as he busted out a back window with the butt of his rifle and began firing.

Rex barked orders, "Petey get over there and give Joey some back-up!"

Petey did as he was told and ran to the rear of the house.

Lester slipped in the garage door, returning from a recon mission.

"There's three of them advancing out back and two in front throwing rocks and dirt clods. Oh yeah, Bert Perkins is perched in a fig tree shooting at us from the south side."

Rex snorted, "He must think he's some kind of sniper. What is he, five feet off the ground?"

Lester laughed. "More like four feet. Anyway, he looked like he was more interested in eating figs than providing cover fire."

Petey shouted, "Man down!"

Rex and Lester turned toward the back window where a shaken Joey covered his face with his hands. Turns out, one of the fourth street boys got off a lucky shot that found its mark on the left lens of Joey's new glasses. The right lens was intact, but the left lens displayed several cracked lines emanating from a pock mark in the middle of the lens.

Handing the glasses back to Joey, Rex gave him a reassuring smile. "You are one lucky cowboy. If you hadn't been wearing your glasses, that shot might have put your eye out."

"But what will I tell my Mother?"

Rex ignored the question. Returning to his firing position, he ordered Joey back to his station with the words, "All you need is one good eye to take care of these bozos."

The battle for Fort Apache was over within the hour. The fourth street boys failed to dislodge the defenders of the fort who lived on second street. After a quickly arranged truce, it was time for a lunch break. Peanut butter, bologna and cheese sandwiches were the hardtack of the two opposing armies. The boys from second and fourth street reveled in their most recent battle, discussing tactics and execution of their respective battle plans as well as the weapons that were used.

T.R. Johannsen, the fourth street Commander, maintained that the pump Daisys were superior to the lever action Red Ryders.

Rex disagreed. "I can fire three shots from my lever action for every shot you get off from the pump."

Licking the frosting off an Oreo, T.R. acknowledged the merits of Rex's logic. "You may be right about that, but when a BB from my pump finds its mark, it hurts a hell of a lot more."

Petey took a long drink from his canteen and wiped his mouth with the sleeve of his Tee shirt. "This is the best Fort Apache ever!"

"Yeah," Lester chimed in. "This the Mother of all Fort Apaches!"

Rex and T.R. looked at each other and nodded in agreement.

T.R. looked at the house that had served as the fort for today's weekend game of war. "No doubt about it, this sure beats those plywood and brush forts we built in the woods."

Bert Perkins unwrapped his second Milky Way bar. "That may be, but this is old man Bartholomew's model home for the new houses he told my daddy he's gonna build on fifth street. I don't reckon he'll be none too happy to see what we've done here today."

T.R.'s eyes narrowed. "Listen up, 'fig-mouth,' you better keep your trap shut or you won't be part of our gang."

Bert quit eating his Milky Way in mid-chew. "I ain't gonna say anything. I just mean . ."

Rex interrupted him. "Listen boys, if we all keep quiet, everything will blow over. We'll stay clear of the house and lay low for a couple of weeks. Then we can build another Fort Apache back in the woods near Frederick's pond."

"Everybody circle up," T.R. replied. The boys of fourth and second street swore an oath of silence regarding the events of the day on pain of death.

Fort Apache's shining moment had come on this fall Saturday morning. No make-shift forts of sticks, branches and scraps of lumber, but a real fort with windows and doors and walls of brick. In fact, the model home was almost a thousand square feet with three bedrooms and a bath and a half and even a single carport. It was built of brick, not like the small two bedroom, one bath, asbestos siding homes of second through fourth streets. Bert Perkins remembered hearing his mother and father talking about the homes that were to be built on Fifth Street. Retrieving a cold, chicken drumstick from the refrigerator, he had heard his father exclaim, "Twenty-one thousand dollars! Who in this neighborhood could ever afford to pay that much for a house?"

*****

Ralph Smith sat next to the window in Mrs. Edge's math class, listening to her drone on about multiplication tables. Glancing out of the window, he saw a sight that made his pulse quicken. A Sheriff's cruiser slid into a parking spot with its blue lights flashing. No siren, just the blue lights. A strange sight no doubt, but Ralph's attention turned to the homework assignment Mrs. Edge was passing out.

She left the room for a moment and returned with Deputy Sheriff Rufus Hightower. Deputy Hightower was well-known to the boys of Milhorn Elementary School. He was the volunteer supervisor of the school's "safety patrol" program. Boys in the fifth and sixth grades who wore the white belts that designated them as members of the safety patrol, helped the younger kids cross the streets to their waiting mothers.

The Deputy Sheriff stood at the front of the class and pulled a rumpled sheet of paper from his shirt pocket and began reading:

"Rex Duggan, T.R. Piercy, Petey McMaster, Joey Donaldson, Lester Cavender, Bert Perkins, Lyle Dove, Stu Solomon, and Dexter Raymond."

When he had finished, the Deputy folded the list of names and returned the sheet of paper to his pocket, simply said: "Come with me."

Ralph looked on with amazement as the boys silently filed out of the room. Realizing that on this occasion the grim finger of justice had passed him by, he wiped a thin bead of sweat from his brow. The only reason he wasn't on that list was because he and his family had been out of town on that fateful weekend.

4

Barefoot Confession

MICHAEL BRASWELL

1958 WAS A YEAR LIKE EVERY OTHER YEAR IN THE YELLOW PINES of South Georgia. Watching three television channels, attending the Baptist church whenever the doors were open, and attending public schools with no air conditioning with others of your ilk, comprised the sacred routines of community life.

I was in my regular spot in Miss Billups sixth grade class, middle of the last row with a window seat. The trick was on the first day of class you had to resist the temptation to lag behind with your buddies and be one of the first kids through the door of home room. There would always be a couple of other girls and boys ahead of you, but you didn't have to worry. They were the serious students who wanted a front row seat. Their motives were clear enough. They wanted to impress the teacher with their enthusiasm and a bit of fawning never hurt when it came grade time. Anything less than an "A" would send them into an emotional tail-spin so a little apple-polishing or as me and my best friend, Freddy, referred to it—"butt-kissing"—provided an extra bit of insurance. Given my "George doesn't live up to his academic potential" reputation resulting from the semi-annual Parent-Teacher conference and my middling grades, the egg-heads always threw a puzzled look my way as if to say, "why aren't you lagging behind with the other Cretins and misanthropes?" Of course, in their haste to suck up to Miss Billups they didn't understand what the prime real estate in the classroom really was, the three magic desks located next to the windows. I always picked the middle one, close enough to the front to avoid the shenanigans in the last row where the trouble-makers and the sullen few resided and where Miss Billups's eagle eye frequently scanned for any sign of impending doom. But not too close to where she might mistake me for one of the butt-kissers frantically waving their arms to answer the next question before she even finished asking it. Yes, the middle desk next to the window was definitely the "magic seat," the place you could gaze out of the window into the great beyond where your imagination rather than sixth grade English could take wing. An occasional well-timed glance at the teacher and nod of the head, feigning interest about what you weren't paying attention to, usually sufficed to maintain a veil of protection that allowed your imagination to sally forth un-abated. Of course, my imagination also made room for Miss Bil-lups, our attractive first-year teacher. At eleven I couldn't explain why or how, but I found my eyes strangely drawn to her. Yes, she was pretty and for several years now there was something about the curve and shape of women that caused me to sit up and take notice. Still, not knowing exactly what to make of such thoughts nor what to do if I did understand them, they only lingered in my young boy's consciousness until the next distraction flew my way.

Today was a repetition of all the other days for the last two weeks. Peering out my window, I watched Old Lady Smithwick carrying groceries she bought at the A&P inside the duplex she shared with her cousin, Jake. There were stories about her and Jake, mostly made up from bits of gossip that floated through the ether-sphere of Hahira, the town I called home. Maybe he was her cousin, maybe he wasn't.

Miss Billups cleared her throat. "Class, I want to introduce you to Willie." She cleared her throat again, as if something was caught in it. "Willie will be joining our class for the remainder of the term."

All eyes turned to the doorway where Willie Jones stood, looking like one of those doomed convicts in a James Cagney movie about to be led to the electric chair. Some classmates stared, others looked away, and the Morgan twins—the first-class assholes that they were—laughed. Willie just stood there like a broke-down field Mule, staring at his dirty, bare feet.

The uncomfortable silence ended when Miss Billups smiled and pointed to a desk in the corner of the back of the room. "There, Willie, you can take that desk."

Columbus had just finished sailing to America when the lunch bell rang. Today's fare was a hard-fried pork chop, string beans, mashed potatoes, and yeast rolls. Lime Jello finished things off for those with a sweet tooth. Two bowls containing a square pound of butter also graced each table, a condiment for the freshly baked bread.

Freddy and I both came from family traditions of fast eaters. Our mothers toiled in their respective kitchens for several hours preparing meals that they considered reasonably wholesome by the standards of the day. Following the example of our fathers, we devoured their efforts in a matter of minutes, often leaving them to finish their meals alone. Rumor had it that Jenny Phillips's family on Fourth Street lingered over their dinners, making small talk and sharing the events of the day with each other. Not so with us. Mealtime was serious business. Other the occasional "pass the cornbread," few words were spoken.

While the other kids attended to their lunches, Freddy and I played "hide the dead fly in the butter." Perhaps, folks in that era were not as hygiene sensitive, but there always seemed to be several dead flies on the floor, courtesy of well-timed swats from the kitchen ladies. Retrieving several of the deceased creatures, like novice sculptors, we would carefully bury them an inch or two below the surface of the butter before smoothing away any trace of their new burial ground. Our reward for our diligence was a scream of surprise and horror from a classmate who spread a dead fly on their bread or better yet, noticed a half-eaten fly on what was left of their roll.

While a pork chop was no meatloaf, the number one ranked lunch-time delicacy, it served its purpose by providing a bit of nourishment and entertainment before afternoon social studies began. Miss Billups' charges mopped up the remnants of their meal, slurping up their lime Jello deserts—all except Willie. Willie sat at the end of his table, two empty seats between him and Nettie Jackson who was known, on occasion, to eat her own boogers. Willie nibbled at the sandwich he had brought wrapped in an old newspaper. He was three dimes short. Three dimes, six nickels or 30 pennies, the price of admission to the cafeteria lunch line.

The hour after lunch was the hardest of the day. Drooping eye-lids and drowsy demeanors called for a nap while Miss Billups called for the answer to what was the capital of Argentina. A spitball whizzed by my face when the teacher turned to write something on the blackboard. I turned to find Freddy rolling another paper bullet. Two rows behind Freddy in the corner sat Willie, eyes closed and tapping his bare feet, keeping time to some secret melody that only he could hear, a silent tune that helped get him through the day.

I didn't notice that Freddy's next spitball had also missed its mark, demonstrating why Freddy never got to pitch in the neighborhood summer baseball games. Instead for some strange reason, I found myself looking out of the corner of my eye at Willie's dirty, bare feet. In interrupting the symmetry of the classroom, the order of what was familiar and predictable, I found myself unable to return to the freedom my desk-side window offered me. Twenty-five students, fifty feet covered by Keds, saddle oxfords, and Buster Brown lace-ups except for one, one boy with no shoes who sat alone away from the others. The picture didn't fit the pattern I had grown accustomed to.

"Supper's ready!" No dinner bell. Just George's mother's shrill announcement that the evening meal was ready. Come one, come all. Me, my younger brother and my father, the honorary head of the household, all hustled to the table. Each in his own way had learned to not keep my mother waiting.

Stew beef, carrots, and potatoes with a side of cooked, canned asparagus casserole comprised the evening banquet. Although my stomach growled, I found myself longing for the overcooked lunchtime pork chop and some cold mashed potatoes. My mother cooked everything "well done"—ham, beef, and chicken—it didn't matter. Everything was dry to the bone. The only time juicy and meat could be used in the same sentence in the Jenkins household was when my father grilled hamburgers outside.

Well-done meat was one thing, but add hardtack gristle to shoe leather tough stew beef and you could chew on the bite you just sawed off for five minutes or more before being able to wash it down with milk. Add a helping of warm, mushy asparagus casserole and you were ready to run and hide. In fact, my younger brother, Elvin, once feigned sickness to dodge the evening meal. After two tablespoons of Castor Oil were administered by our mother, Elvin never used that tactic again, dutifully gnawing on the contents of the plate set before him.

Homework finished, shower taken, and teeth more or less brushed, I was getting my clothes ready for another school day. Wiping down my black canvas, white rubber-soled Keds, Willie and his bare feet took center stage in my mind's eye once more. I wasn't certain why. After all, I was just a typical eleven-year-old boy. Still, the thought of Willie as the only person in class with no shoes lingered. I thought to himself, "Nothing wrong with bare feet in general." Me and Freddy and our pals often went barefoot during long, hot summer vacations. But that was different. Miss Billups's class wasn't summer vacation and being shoeless in it didn't fit the order of the day.

I stuck my head out of my bedroom door. "Hey Mom."

Mildred Jenkins put the pan she was drying down, walked into her oldest son's bedroom and crossed her arms. "What in the world are you looking for in the bottom of that filthy closet? You should be in bed. Tomorrow's a school day."

Pulling a pair of white buck Sunday shoes I had outgrown out of the closet, I held them up. "Can I give these shoes to a kid at school?"

"Why would you do that?" my mother replied.

"Because he's the only kid in our class that comes to school barefooted."

She unfolded her arms and put her hands in her apron pockets. "And that bothers you?"

"Well, yes. I reckon it does."

My Mother's expression softened. "Well, that's a good thing. You can put them in the brown paper sack I saved from grocery shopping."

What does a young boy say to someone he doesn't really know at the beginning of recess when he hands him a brown paper bag with a pair of slightly used white bucks in it?

He says, "Here . . . I thought maybe you could use these."

Opening the bag, Willie peered inside.

I mumbled something along the lines of "I don't know if they will fit, but . . . "

I didn't finish the rest of the sentence because the lost, dull countenance that had previously isolated Willie from everyone he came in contact with was transformed in the blinking of an eye into a different person. It was the first time I had seen Willie smile. Actually, Willie didn't smile, his whole face turned into a spotlight of happiness. He was so excited, he almost looked as though he might start dancing. Willie kept saying over and over, "Thank you. Thank you. Thank you."

Although it didn't look that way to me, Willie exclaimed that the shoes fit perfectly.

That was the good news.

The bad news was Willie began following me around at recess. Each morning and afternoon, he would stand aside at a respectful distance, watching me and my friends play together.

People began to talk.

I began to feel the heat.

First looks, then whispers and finally, my circle of friends began to grow smaller.

Then one day, I turned to Willie and said the fateful words, "Quit following me around."

A simple enough phrase, direct and to the point. When the words tumbled out of my mouth, the spell was broken. What was left of Willie's desperate, hesitant smile vanished and he became invisible once more. I returned to my eleven-year-old world and the friends I was used to and Willie disappeared.

I was a boy then. Now, sixty years later, I still remember. I once gave a barefoot boy a pair of white buck shoes—when what he needed was a friend.

5

Justice Wore an Apron

Anthony Cavender

In the nineteen fifties and sixties, "Wait until your Daddy gets home" was a declaration that made a misbehaving boy's blood run cold. For most of the families in my neighborhood, fathers were the dispensers of justice which usually meant a whipping with a switch, paddle, belt, or whatever was conveniently at hand. On less frequent occasions when infractions were more severe, a "whupping" was administered, stopping somewhere short of life's end.

Parents justified whippings biblically, resorting to Proverbs 13:24, which in its abbreviated form is "Spare the rod, spoil the child." After being tormented all day with "wait until your Daddy gets home," kids waited in fearful anticipation of their father's arrival, all the while desperately thinking about how they could conjure up some kind of magical negotiation skill that would spare them the inevitable whipping that was to come. In my family, things were different. My mother was the primary disciplinarian, the judge and the jury and when the guilty verdict came in, the sole dispenser of punishment. Although this may have been the case in a few other families, in most households the wielder of the rod of justice was the man of the house, also known by some awaiting their fate as the "grim reaper."

In many ways, Mama was a woman ahead of her time. My parents argued about many things, but mainly over Mama's desire to work outside the home. She was an accomplished secretary, typed 120 words a minute with no errors, and early in her marriage she worked as the executive secretary to the president of the Werthan Bag Corporation in Nashville. After giving birth to the first of five children, my father decided that she should not go back to work. Perhaps, he felt that her working diminished his image as a provider which was a key element of a man's self-worth in the fifties or maybe he feared her having more freedom. Mama had been a "flapper" in her younger days and was unconventional by nature. She was also something of a romantic, sometimes fantasizing about being Isadora Duncan, riding in a convertible down the Champs-Elysees with her scarf flying in the air. She was a woman born at the wrong time, saddled with five children, and denied the freedom to have a life outside the home. She had ample opportunity to take out the frustration born of an unfulfilled life in disciplining her children, especially her impudent sons, but she didn't. Her artistic instincts may have borne fruit with the creative forms of punishment, but she was always fair.

When I was five years old, playing with my next-door-neighbor, J.R. Thomas, age nine, he and I discovered several bags of concrete his father, a building contractor, had stored in the basement. For some reason, possibly possession by the Devil, we ripped the bags open and gleefully threw handfuls of concrete mix at each other. It was quite a sight. We chased each other, laughing and screaming, slinging concrete, just having a really good time when we were suddenly interrupted by J.R.'s mother. The air was thick with dust, torn bags were scattered all over the floor, and we looked like a couple of extras from the movie, "Night of the Living Dead." She made a quick assessment of the situation as mothers tend to do and told me to go home. Turning to J.R., I heard her say,

"I'll show this mess to your Daddy when he gets home." Later that afternoon while playing in the driveway that separated our houses, I heard J.R. and his father talking through the open basement window. J.R. cried, "Please, please, don't whip me." He offered a final plaintive plea that he was sorry, that I was the instigator, and that he would clean everything up. Mr. Thomas said nothing and slipped his belt off—I could almost feel the quiver of the leather as he pulled it through the loops of his pants. I heard him tell J.R. to bend over and with a final fatherly admonition, proceeded to whack him across his butt and legs. The pop of the belt when it struck J.R. made the hair on the back of my neck stand up. I imagined his pain with every stroke of the belt.

Suddenly, the thought occurred to me: "What if his father could see me through the window and possibly come for me next to take my turn with the lash?" I started running for the house, but abruptly stopped with an even more frightening thought: "What if Mrs. Thomas had called my mother and reported the concrete fight with J.R?" If so, I was in big trouble, but not with my father because, unlike every family I knew in our neighborhood, I would not have to wait until Daddy came home from work to receive justice. My chances of evading Mama were about as good as a slug's in a saltbox. It was as though she was psychic and had eyes in the back of her head. Still, I did my best. I tried to sneak into the house through the kitchen. Holding my breath, I quietly closed the outside door. When I turned around, I found her sitting at the table drinking a cup of coffee. She gave me a once-over with her eyes and said that she had just got off the phone with Mrs. Thomas. Before she could finish telling me about her conversation with J.R.'s Mom, I went for a preemptive strike, blaming J.R. with a full-throated gusto. Yes ma'am, J.R. had definitely started it and I was only defending myself. Mind you, I was fully aware that I had been caught in a lie so many times before about other misadventures that there was no possibility of her believing anything I said. Moreover, she had also successfully dealt with my two older brothers in the past, both masters of prevarication and casuistry. My sisters, Betty Anne and Maria, both older, rarely suffered a whipping, not because Mama discriminated against boys, but because for some strange reason, they seldom got into trouble. Mama casually got up from her chair, opened a kitchen counter drawer, and pulled out a spatula, which she called the "pancake turner." Then, with the swiftness of a Ninja warrior, she grabbed me by the arm and proceeded to whip me with it. In anticipation of each strike, I moved a little forward to diminish the impact, but she kept right in stride. As I mentioned before, she had been a dancer and knew all my moves, the spatula keeping time with my tap dance of pain. Truthfully, the pancake turner didn't hurt all that much. It was the shame of the thing that hurt most.

Without Mama's judicial interventions, there's little doubt that, if left to my own devices, I would have ended up on what she called "the other side of life" and become a criminal, or worse, a Republican. Simply put, like my older brothers, I needed to be controlled.

There was the time I set the back yard on fire playing with matches. There's something mesmerizing about matches, fire, and a young boy's imagination. The dry Bermuda grass burned fast, propelled by a strong breeze. The fire moved rapidly into the next-door neighbor's yard where it smoked some sheets hanging on a clothesline. A playful prank quickly turned into a four-alarm catastrophe. I ran into the house and exclaimed to Mama that I had seen a little boy from down the street playing with matches and that he had set our yard on fire. She smoothed out her apron, pulled the pancake turner from the drawer and replied, "I think I know that little boy and he's standing right in front of me."

There was also another occasion when I pretended to drive the family car, a huge barge of a car, a 1954 Pontiac Eight. With my imagination running amok, I inadvertently shifted it out of park. Unfortunately, the handbrake wasn't engaged and the car began to roll backward. I hopped out and watched helplessly as it rolled down the driveway, across the street, over a ditch, finally coming to rest just a few feet from a neighbor's house. I tried mightily, but couldn't think of a plausible lie to get out of the situation, so I simply went in the house and told my parents what I had done.

Mother was favorably impressed with my candor, but not enough to avoid another session with what I came to call "Mr. Pancake Turner."

Although not successful, I should have received an "A" for effort as I continued to try outmaneuvering my mother. She asked me once to go outside and bring back a switch for a whipping. Instead, I drug in a limb that had fallen from an old hackberry tree. It was huge, longer than I was tall, and full of dead leaves and twigs. My thinking was that she would find it too unwieldy to use and thus give up on the notion of whipping me. Instead, to my astonishment, she picked up the tree limb with both hands and clumsily thrashed the entire backside of my body with it. It didn't hurt that much because it was, as I figured, hard to handle. Still, watching Mama attempt to thrash me with that limb was a bit unnerving. On another occasion, I determined if I could remove her favorite instrument of justice, "Mr. Pancake Turner," she would be less inclined to whip me or possibly give up whipping me altogether. It was nothing less than a stealth operation as I buried "Mr. Pancake Turner" in the back yard. The problem was that I failed to bury it deep enough. It was soon discovered when it got tangled in the blades of the push mower for which, of course, I received a spanking, this time by hand. Although I wasn't a quick learner, in time I learned not to trifle with her.

Looking back, I think I acquired a deep sense of fairness from my mother. She believed in being fair with all people, regardless of their social status, ethnicity, or race. She was a champion of the underdog, a Roosevelt Democrat to the core, and an advocate of civil rights long before the riots and sit-ins. When I was five or six, I rode downtown on a bus with Mama. She took me to the dentist and then to see a movie, "The High and the Mighty." I noticed, as I had before, that the negroes (an acceptable and considered polite term for black men and women during that time) on the bus had to sit at the back. I asked her why? She didn't bother with explaining racism. How could she? She simply said: "It's not fair. It shouldn't be this way." She befriended many black people during her life, but one in particular, Erlene, was a genuine friend, as genuine as such relationships were possible. She hired Erlene every spring to help with deep cleaning the house, which always included the tedious task of stripping and waxing the floors. Two vivid memories of mine are Mama and Erlene together on their hands and knees scrubbing the floors and applying Jubilee floor wax. The other was the two of them working at dual ironing boards while listening to Nashville's black radio station, WVOL. Mother was especially fond of rhythm and blues and country music, especially the maudlin songs of Hank Williams and as far as she was concerned, Frank Sinatra hung the moon. I also recall the day, several years later, when Mama got all dressed up and attended the graduation of one of Erlene's daughters from Tennessee State University.

My mother's sense of fairness and fair play was also evident in her role as dispenser of justice. More often than not, she issued a verbal reprimand for the first offense, a kind of judicial probation that clearly established a boundary. A second offense warranted a whipping. A case in point was an incident involving a Red Ryder BB gun and my two older brothers, Buddy and Wayne, who had been told more than once not to shoot at a person. Buddy, the oldest, fired the gun at a can in the garage and the bb ricocheted off it and hit Wayne in the stomach. Buddy asked Wayne if it hurt? When Wayne said no, he shot him again, but this time at close range. Wayne screamed in pain when he was hit and ran into the house crying. He told mother what happened and she promptly went to the garage and confronted Buddy. His defense was that he was only experimenting to determine the power of the gun. She took the BB gun from him and told him to stand against the garage door. Mama then proceeded to shoot him twice. It was all very Old Testament, eye-for-an-eye stuff, but also a lesson about picking on vulnerable people. Worst of all from Buddy's and Wayne's perspective, she quarantined the Red Ryder for a couple of weeks.

There were fathers in our neighborhood who seemed to relish whipping their children. Capricious and brutal, they looked for excuses and on occasion, made up violations which allowed them to vent their personal frustrations and anger on their children. Perhaps, their motivations came from their own sense of inadequacy

34

or inability to cope with life's challenges. They also played favorites. They might punish one child severely for an offense and then punish a sibling lightly or not at all for the very same or similar offense. I even knew schoolmates who served as their fathers' "whipping boys." We used the term "mean" to describe these fathers, as in "Mr. Cline is a mean man," but we also called them "assholes." Fortunately, my mother was not a mean disciplinarian. She set clear and explicit boundaries, followed precedence, and administered punishment fairly to all her children.

Although only five-feet-two with a slight build, my mother was indomitable and fearless, especially when it came to the defense of her children and the family's reputation. Sometimes it was embarrassing to witness her give someone, as she expressed it, "a piece of her mind." Although well-read, highly articulate and in command of an impressive vocabulary, when angry, she could get blue with the best of them. Her children, of course, were not allowed to curse or use profanity, and when we did, she washed our mouths out with soap. She also liked to drink beer, but we couldn't drink it until we were eighteen. Like most parents, Mama was a hypocrite about many things, but we had to live by her dictum: "Do as I say, not as I do."

More than once I took advantage of Mama's fearlessness, like the time when I called on her to defend me and my best friend, Ralph, against Ralph's brother, Jerry. Ralph and I built a treehouse and shed in an isolated wooded area not far from my parents' house. We constructed our crudely built structures from bits and pieces of scrap lumber from nearby home construction sites. Some of the materials we deemed "scrap" could in the eyes of some, possibly be described as new. No doubt, we should have been punished. It's called stealing.

The site served as the headquarters of our club, the "Red Devils." In the shed, we had a cache of walnuts and hedge apples that we used in our ongoing war with a rival club, the "Black Satans." One day Jerry came to check out our site, and that's when the trouble began. Jerry was an imposing fifteen-year-old boy-man who stood six-feet-two and weighed around 180 hundred pounds.

He was known in school as a "hood" and skilled street fighter. It is worth noting that Jerry also had the highest IQ in his class, a fact that he took no pride in. We along with many other neighborhood kids were afraid of him. It didn't take long for Jerry to discover our cache of walnuts and hedge apples. He first started throwing walnuts at us. We sought refuge in the treehouse and it served us well until he resorted to throwing hedge apples. The force of his throw and the size of the hedge apples were too much for the flimsy treehouse walls which quickly fell apart, leaving us completely exposed. As we scurried from the confines of our treehouse, Jerry continued to pelt us with hedge apples. One of them found its mark squarely in my back and knocked the wind out of me. Somehow I managed to get myself together as Jerry continued his assault. I ran home and told Mama what had happened. The look in her eyes said it all—a storm of justice was brewing. With me in tow she went to the treehouse and confronted Jerry face-to-face. She began her interrogation by asking him why he enjoyed picking on kids half his size. Shifting uneasily, he replied that he was only having some fun and meant no harm. Picking up a handful of hedge apples, she said, "Is this fun?" Mama followed her question with a fast-ball right into his chest from a distance of four feet. She then hit him with another hedge apple as he began to back away, and another between his shoulder blades as he picked up his pace toward home. Of course, Jerry was in no position to retaliate, but I was never prouder of my mother than in that moment.

For several years, I wondered why Daddy left the task of physical punishment to my mother. Later when I turned twenty or so, I asked him. He said that when he was sixteen he made a stand against his father who was preparing to beat him for a minor transgression involving loading produce on a wagon. This was around 1922. He told his father that if he laid a hand on him he would regret it. The old man ignored his warning and moved in, so my father knocked him down with his fist, and followed with several more blows. After that, the beatings stopped. I never knew my grandfather, but I speculate now that the punishment he inflicted was at times severe and entailed flesh on flesh: slaps, punches, and kicks. After enduring several beatings, my father resolved to have nothing to do with any form of physical punishment, yet, interestingly, he did not stand in the way of his wife whipping their children. I'm sure he would have stepped in had she been excessive, but she never was, and though they had a contentious relationship, they were always of one mind when it came to rearing their children.

The whippings ceased when I turned nine or ten, even though I remained an imperfect son well into adolescence. My parents transitioned to other forms of punishment like withholding allowance, labor, and grounding, but they were, in my estimation, always fair in application. Whenever I left the house, Mama and Daddy often said, "Be a good boy." I knew exactly what they meant. I fondly recall the letters I received from Mama and Daddy when I left Nashville for Knoxville to attend graduate school. They always ended with the admonition, "Be a good boy." I regret now putting Mama in the position of having to discipline me because she didn't enjoy doing it. I've striven to be a "good boy" and have often fallen short, but I carry Mama's sense of fairness and fair play deep within me. I became an anthropologist, and like many in my profession I'm unapologetic in my advocacy of cultural relativism and social justice. As Wendell Berry put it, "Rats and roaches live by competition under the law of supply and demand; it is the privilege of human beings to live under the laws of justice and mercy." Mama would surely agree.

6

I Spy

RALPH BLAND

LIKE EVERYONE ELSE WHO LIVED AT THE BOTTOM OF THE HILL, I could stand in my front yard on summer evenings after dinner in those long ago days and listen to Marsha Webb sing from her open kitchen window as she washed her dishes at the top of Carter Drive. It was said—although no one ever confirmed it—that Marsha Webb once had sung in the opera back in Omaha before moving south with her husband to our town. On those evenings after supper it seemed she couldn't help but keep her vocal instrument tuned by singing those melodies with Italian lyrics we couldn't understand in a pure and clear soprano we had all come to recognize and rather enjoy in spite of ourselves and our inability to comprehend what they were about. I was thirteen then in that summer of 1963, and though inclined toward immaturity and random acts only a piss-ant would engage in, I was still in touch enough with the world around me to acknowledge a beautiful sound when I heard it.

I'm fairly certain everybody in the neighborhood was a little like that. We were the families of working-class Southerners raised on the music of Top Forty and the Grand Ole Opry, but once Marsha Webb moved in and began to wash her dishes in her kitchen at the top of Carter Drive she was officially a part of the neighborhood. The music that floated down from her window soon became a part of us too.

Marvin and Marsha Webb, late of Nebraska, had two children, Charles and Pamela. Pamela was two years younger than me. She was skinny, wore black-rimmed glasses and carried a flute around in a brown case back and forth to school. I don't think I remember a single time I saw Pamela without that flute case entrenched in her fingers like it was the most important possession on the face of the earth. I'm not saying that being a flutist was all that terrible a thing or anything like that. Heck, for all I know old Pamela could have gone on from those apprentice days to being first chair in the Symphony or something, maybe even landing a gig as that person who played the solo flute in the middle of "California Dreamin'" with the Mamas and Papas, or perhaps tutoring Ian Anderson on how to blow those vicious vibes with Jethro Tull. I mean, stranger things have happened.

Charles on the other hand, I remember well. I could write a James Michener saga about him if I thought anyone would read it. He was fifteen that summer, two years older than me or any of the other kids who lived nearby. Given his seniority, the rest of us couldn't help but watch his actions and listen to the words that came out of his mouth, absorbing his offerings like oxygen and the gospel truth even though a part of us knew what Charles brought to us was nothing close to the truth. It didn't occur to our pack of wild and impressionable pre-teens that the reason Charles was always around as an elder statesman for all our games and secret trysts was because his act had already worn thin with the boys his own age. In fact, his actions had already led the majority of his peers to scorn him. They came to view him as a goofball, a weirdo who was never going to grow out of it and take a step into the circle of legitimate high school social acceptance, whatever the hell that was.

I'd usually discover Charles in my yard on those summer mornings, shooting basketball in my driveway because I had the most level court of any one, unless you wanted to walk a half-mile to the elementary school playground. Even then, my court was preferred to the school because it had a net rather than just an iron rim. For wannabee NBA stars, it was important to hear that swishing sound when the ball passed through for two points.

With no school or job or any pressing place to be that summer, I generally stayed up late watching television and slept until about nine a.m. Most mornings I was awakened from my sleep-induced comas by the sound of a ball dribbling on the asphalt driveway and Charles's own voice providing commentary for the epic battle the two imaginary teams in his head with only him as both a participant and spectator.

"Peterson dribbles outside, hands it off to Taylor. Taylor goes inside, wants to shoot, but Oliver's all over him. Taylor finds Kelly over in the left corner. Twenty-two foot shot, and it's good! What a shot by Kelly and it's all tied up again!"

I would often amble out to the back porch and watch these titanic struggles in my pajamas. Other than the fact the entire scene was maniacal in its convolutedness and scope, I still had to marvel most of the time at how good and adept Charles Webb was at this schizophrenic tilt. If you watched him for a while and listened in and sort of suspended your disbelief, you could almost see what he was seeing.

He was like that in a lot of things. What was actually happening in the world and what was going on in his head were never necessarily the same. Maybe that was the reason Charles could never find a spot with the older crowd he was supposed to be hanging around with. Maybe he just couldn't quite turn the corner on putting away the baseball cards and the bicycles and moving on to the world of grown-up girls and hot cars and whose party you were invited to on Saturday night.

He'd finally spot me on my porch and act like the performance I had just witnessed was no big deal. To Charles, the bizarre things he did on a daily basis was as natural as waking up in the morning.

"What are you doing today?" he'd always ask to determine if I'd change my routine for something really important he had in mind.

"I don't know," I would say. "I thought I might go to the Y or maybe go fishing at the pond."

The pond was this little offshoot of water that ran off from the river a couple of miles away. It was about four feet deep during the rainy season and if you were lucky you might catch a fish about the side of your bird finger. Mostly we'd load up our line with biscuit dough as bait and catch fish slightly bigger than minnows, which we would throw back in the pond hoping somehow they'd grow and get larger.

"It's too hot to fish," Charles would assure me. "Whatever fish are in that pond are just gonna lay on the bottom. To catch those guys during the summer, you either have to get there early or go late when the sun isn't so hot."

It was true Charles had always been the best fisherman among of any of us boys, so I took his fishing prognosis to be the absolute truth.

"I'll tell you what I'm going to do today." He lowered his voice so no one within miles could hear and squinted up at me conspiratorially. "After lunch I'm going back to where I was yesterday and do the same thing I did then all over again. Shoot, I may go every day for the rest of this summer as long as the sun's up there shining."

I gave him a puzzled look. "I don't know what you're talking about."

"I'm talking about how if you walk through the back of my yard and go out past the dog pen in the Crowder's yard, you come to a big wooden privacy fence. Do you know who that fence belongs to?"

"I think that's where Tommy and Linda Carlisle live."

"That's absolutely right. But did you happen to know that every afternoon after lunch Linda and a whole bunch of her friends—Susan Cooper and Judy Daniels and a couple more—like to sunbathe out there in the backyard? Sometimes there's five or six girls out there. I'm here to tell you most of the time none of them are wearing a whole lot of clothes. I know because I've been watching them lay around on blankets and lawn chairs for about a week now."

He began to smile at me in that crazy way he often resorted to when he wanted to make a point. Any second I expected him to start laughing like he was Dracula's henchman, Renfield, which was another one of his traits that I figured was denying him entrance into the world of high school where he truly belonged.

I couldn't, however, turn down the opportunity to view an unclad Linda Carlisle and the legions of sisterhood that accompanied her. Linda and her friends were three and four years older than me. Some of them were cheerleaders who mostly dated big and burly football players while I was just a junior-high jerk who'd never even touched a girl and wouldn't have known what to do if I did. About the only thing I'd ever had to do with the opposite sex at that point was to dare to imagine what in real life one of these creatures might possibly look like naked. I mean, I'd looked at some Playboy magazines a couple of times, but I hadn't really lingered over the centerfolds too much because they were all about as unreal, other-worldly and frightening as any of the older girls I saw at school or church. The times my mother forced me to attend church, me being the low and vile sinner that I was, I didn't know who to fear the most, an angry Jehovah or these girls with lips and breasts and legs that I knew would one day cast me into oblivion. I knew I was doomed either way.

"You want to come with me?" he asked.

I shook my head up and down like a puppet.

"Yeah," I said.

I got a lot better at it as the summer went along, but on that first afternoon of my spying career my stealth abilities were about as non-existent as my knowledge of the female species. I don't know if it was a result of my impending excitement, but it seemed like anytime I could find a hole to step in or a tree limb to smack me in the face or a root to trip over I was successful in maiming myself enough to cause a thud or elicit a highly audible gasp of pain. While most older guys would have been pissed at all these possible interruptions during so delicate an undertaking, Charles seemed to find that these faux pas added to the dangerousness of our mission and thus appeared to thrive on the possibility we might get discovered. I guess you could say he enjoyed living on the edge.

"We're almost there," he said, leaning against a tree. "We have to go about twenty more yards, so we've got to be really quiet from here on out. You just stay behind me and I'll show you where to stop."

On the brink of completing this hazardous task, I prepared myself for my first journey into the mysterious and mystical world of female anatomical observations. My heart beat like "Wipeout" was being played on seventy-eight speed. My breathing became rapid and heavy. I had never felt like this before.

I looked down at my feet to make certain I wasn't going to trip again at so crucial a time, and there on the toe of my right tennis shoe sat a lizard with a purple tail and a yellow stripe down his back who looked like he might have been one of those Komodo Dragons that enjoyed swallowing their prey whole. I forgot in an instant the lure of the barely clad cheerleaders on the other side of the privacy fence. Instead I started slinging my leg like I was kicking off for the Green Bay Packers in an effort to get the reptile in question off of me before he advanced up my leg inside my shorts. All of this sudden physical activity not only caused me to kick Charles in the butt, but also resulted in me loudly kicking the privacy fence and announcing our presence to the possibly naked contingent on the other side—that the perverts had arrived and they had best start covering themselves up and phoning for the police.

The next thing I knew I was running away from the scene as fast as I could, running from the lizard I was sure had a forked tongue and was seeking me out, and running from the awful possibility of capture and punishment for being discovered. Worse than that, I feared becoming forever known for the rest of my sorry life as one of those dirty boys who looked at girls through the slats of a wooden fence because he wasn't good enough to get to look at one up close on a real life date.

We were never sure if the sun-bathing beauties had heard us on that day or not, but we decided the wisest thing we could do was to not revisit the scene of the crime for a while and allow suspicions to die down a bit before daring to attempt such a deed again. "We'll give it a couple of weeks," Charles told me, "and then they'll forget all about it. It's a long summer and we'll have plenty of opportunities to go back. Besides, they're not the only ones to see around here."

He was right. Over the next two weeks and well past July the fourth, we stayed busy spying on the houses around us and the people who lived inside them. Most of the time our visual eavesdropping was harmless enough. We would listen to housewives chat in their driveways while hiding behind tall hedges. We would climb a tree and watch women work in their gardens in what they thought was their private backyards. Walking down the aisles in grocery stores, we would watch people shop so we'd know what they were having for supper that evening. At the YMCA pool we could swim around catching snatches of conversations and try to construct a meaning for what was going on in each of these stranger's lives. We were anonymous and invisible. Without this world and its everyday drama, there was nothing to be had on our own. We were as devoid of individual skills or interests as the invisible summer wind that blew in our face.

With all the experience I was garnering from my new hobby, I found myself becoming more confident and emboldened with each new endeavor. Like Charles, I began to enjoy the thrill of locating a new target or staking out a fresh territory where the next adventure of life might come my way. I liked the unpredictability of the subject matter, of having such a profound interest in the goings-on of strangers and those neighbors in close proximity who had never bothered to learn my name. It was like I had been granted a power for going through my identity-free life so weak and defenseless to this point. I finally felt I had obtained some measure of control.

I became so fearless that I began to go out on my own without Charles along as a mentor. Granted, I was perhaps not as imaginative or creative in these endeavors without Charles's wild bursts of inspiration and bravado. Still, I was able to inject my sensibilities into church when I got hauled there or the doctor's office where I got my allergy shots and around my own house. Sometimes after supper, I'd go outside on the pretense of seeing my friends and instead sneak across the street to peek through a side window and see what the Watsons were having to eat that night. I would spy to my heart's content while listening to Marsha Webb's soprano lilting down from the top of Carter Drive. It was as if her voice was a partner in my high and secret crimes.

July passed and our spying expeditions began to lose their flavor, mostly because by then we had looked in every nook and cranny and turned over every promising rock in our vicinity in our zealousness to unearth every secret about the world around us. With the absence of an automobile to transport us to new locales, our spying began to become like the summer reruns on television. It was getting boring watching the same old thing over and over again and I found myself silently wishing for Labor Day and the new school year that would begin the following day.

I was almost to the point where I halfway wished school would hurry up and start. Of course, school meant I would have to be out in the world to answer roll call and be visible and vulnerable to whatever havoc the stream of everyday life might want to send my way. I also had to consider the advantage of not having anything to do and a stretch of time where my presence was not required, to be a blessing I would one day covet and wish like hell, I could return to. I told myself it was better to languish this way than to become rigidly embroiled in a real life situation I could not for the life of me escape from.

I was weighing these possibilities one night after supper. It was a night when all the usual suspects of my spying agenda held no interest for me. The idea of going and finding Charles to lead me in a new adventure and locale seemed troublesome and unpromising—almost irritating. I seemed to have arrived at a point where Charles's stories and plans were beginning to not be so entertaining. Perhaps, I was getting old like the summer and was reaching that plateau Charles's classmates had already arrived at, where it was time to get over into the passing lane and move around Charles Webb puttering along in his funny little boy's world. I knew I was going to have to soon start avoiding Charles. It was becoming clearer each day that I no longer wanted to be a spectator involved in the events of his imaginative life. I was getting too old for him.

I was starting to think there had never been any half-naked cheerleaders on the other side of the Carlisle fence.

Most of these thoughts came my way after dinner, when I stood at the edge of my driveway, looking up Carter Drive. I held a whiffle-ball bat on my shoulder and from time to time, tossed up a piece of gravel and hit it down the road. I had the game all figured out, what constituted a single, what was a double or a triple, and how far the rock had to travel for it to be a home run. I liked hitting those rocks all over the place like I was a big league slugger, but I never said anything about it out loud. I kept that much to myself. I just liked the way the hollow bat made its noise when the rock flew off it and how watching those rocks sail away gave me time to think.

One night in the middle of batting practice I had this idea of how I could break out of the rut I'd fallen into and do something off the wall. I thought how great it would be to turn the tables on Charles. After all, hadn't he been spying on everybody in the county most of the summer? The next day was Labor Day and after that we'd all be back in school, and all I'd be able to say is I'd wiled away an entire summer accomplishing nothing. Summers were hard to come by even at my age, and now all the blame for my lack of accomplishments seemed to point to Charles Webb. Maybe, I reckoned, I should declare my independence from him by giving him a dose of his own medicine.

Besides, it could be fun.

Marsha Webb had stopped singing when I started up the hill. On this particular day the sun was beginning to set in contrast with the long summer days already past. The twilight felt good on my crew-cut in place of the hot sun that had scorched my head for months. I heard Cricket, the Anderson's Chihuahua, yapping from her fenced-in yard, but since Cricket barked all the time anyway I didn't think anyone would take any particular notice of me passing this way. I crossed over to the Pearson's side yard and walked around to the back where the Webb's backyard began. There was a shed back there where I knew Marvin Webb kept his tools and lawnmower. From there I snuck around the side of the house to where I could get a look at the window of Charles's room. I wanted to catch him doing something he didn't want anybody in the world to ever know about.

I heard voices as I skulked by the downstairs den door and couldn't help but stop dead in my tracks and listen. Marvin Webb talking—yelling, actually—and every now and then I could hear Marsha Webb emit what amounted to a child-like, strangled whimper from that throat that recently had engulfed our neighborhood in song.

Then came the sounds of slaps. One, two, then a brief pause before the third slap, the loudest of them all.

For a long moment I stood there like a statue, immobile and silent, afraid to move for fear Marvin Webb would discover my uninvited presence in his yard. I was afraid to run away because to do so meant I could never look Charles Webb in the eye again. I could never look down my nose on his pose of perpetual childhood. Why should he grow up? Why should I or anyone else grow up because after you do, you have to come to grips with shit like this? Afraid and frightened beyond words, I finally broke and ran from their yard. I knew I would have to carry the notion that life was always going to come at me in layers just like this, that what was a beautiful song on the surface was never going to stay that way for me or anyone else for very long. I would know from now on there was always going to be a bruise or a sob somewhere beneath the surface of everything I saw.

It took me a while to muster up enough courage to get back down the hill. I went in the house and watched television for a while with my parents although I couldn't tell you anything about what was on for the life of me. All I know is I went to bed and the next morning I awoke to the sound of Charles playing basketball outside. By the sound of his voice he was involved in another exciting game. It was like what went on the night before had changed nothing.

And on that Labor Day and for all the twilights following, I looked in no more windows after finishing my supper. I ceased listening to voices in other rooms. I grew to care very little what people were doing outside my own personal sphere. Instead I stood at the edge of my driveway with my tan plastic bat, hitting rocks over imaginary fences while Marsha Webb sang what must have been one of the saddest songs on earth in a faraway voice that was hers alone.

7

Invisible Boy

MICHAEL BRASWELL

ALTHOUGH WAVY BLOND HAIR AND CLEAR BLUE EYES GAVE TEDDY a strange sort of handsome, "five foot two, eyes of blue" was not a description that lived up to a teenage boy's testosterone dreams. To make matters worse, Teddy was not a particularly good name for a fifteen-year-old boy of slight build trying to prove his mettle in a one-street, blue-collar subdivision. And if his name and physique weren't enough of a handicap, his family's well-worn singlewide trailer stood out like a sore thumb in the sea of split-foyer, ranch and two-story stick-built houses.

While the adults in the neighborhood weren't about to roll out the red carpet for the trailer family perched on a kind of no-man's land in a cornfield just on edge of the subdivision's boundary, they had just enough decency to accommodate to some extent, the family's lonely son.

Teddy's story was originally told to Little Jack, the neighborhood renegade and closest thing to a friend Teddy would ever have. His story filtered its way from Little Jack's parents to the Smiths then the Johnsons and on to the Bartholomews until everyone in the neighborhood had heard it at least twice, everyone except old man Murphy who stayed to himself in a vinyl-clad split-foyer ever since his wife Norma died.

Of course, as Teddy's story made its way through the various families, it took on a number of twists and turns, exaggerations both added and subtracted. The gist of it is as follows: When Teddy was eight years old, his Daddy drank whiskey and beat and abused his mother while he and his younger sister were forced to watch. When in a drunken state, his father was fond of threatening to do his mother, sister and himself in with his good friends, Smith and Wesson. Weary of his relentless abuse, Teddy's mother decided to turn his father's friends against him.

Three times these friends spoke his name and three times stunned, he watched the red, concentric holes appear on his midsection. He only uttered one word during the entire ordeal and he only said it once. After the first shot rang out, he shouted, "Teddy!"

Teddy and his sister looked on in silence as their father fell against the living room wall and slid down it, clutching what was left of his Bud-Lite and watching its contents mingle with the blood pouring from his belly onto the shag carpet.

Two years later, Teddy's mother married his current stepfather and two years after that they moved onto no-man's land.

Although Teddy and his mother had never spoken of the killing, and as much as he believed in his own mind that his father deserved what he got, one thing had always bothered him about the incident. He didn't like the way his dying father spoke to him. He didn't like being called by name as if he were some kind of official witness—as if he could have done something about the shooting. If Teddy hadn't been called out by his dying Daddy, he could have remained invisible. Of course, to the parents in the neighborhood, he was still for the most part invisible, but not so much that they wouldn't invite him in when he knocked on their front doors looking for refuge and a prospective playmate.

Still, the welcome mats, one after another, were eventually withdrawn because Teddy—like anyone dying of an unquenchable thirst—couldn't stop drinking from any sign of friendship and kindness that was offered, no matter how small or fragile. So on he went, from one house and playmate to another. As he searched for the next sign of hospitality, what he left behind looked like a clear-cut forest. Whatever his circumstance, no matter how many doors were closed to him and how few were open, there was always one place Teddy was accepted or at least tolerated—the basketball court at the end of the street.

In the cul-de-sac on Muskgrove Lane, a portable basketball goal and backboard stood guard like a silent sentinel and waited. Around three-thirty each fall afternoon, Monday through Friday, you could hear it coming before you saw it. An ancient yellow school bus slowly belched its way down the single curved road of Muskgrove Lane and expelled its prisoners, free until six forty-five the following morning.

They came out of that bus like rats leaving a sinking ship— first grade through high school. The youth of the neighborhood sauntered and ran toward the houses that beckoned them with the promise of snacks and juice. Thirty minutes later, the rhythmic thumping of basketballs sounded like a war chant and signaled that the games were about to begin.

Younger boys watched older ones dribble basketballs between their legs, make fancy lay-up shots and attempt the occasional but rarely successful, dunk. Boys and the several girls who braved the hallowed court raised their hands and voices, begging to be picked. But their cries to be chosen fell on deaf ears. To the older boys of Muskgrove Lane, they had been designated the Peanut Gallery, spectators one and all—spectators not players. Nothing more needed to be said. The best the members of the Peanut Gallery could hope for Monday through Friday was the brief window of opportunity that presented itself between games. Their reward for being loyal and appreciative spectators was the possibility of five minutes of wild abandon on the court while the real players took a water break at the end of each game. The brief melee only faintly resembled the game of basketball.

Although Teddy was old enough to qualify as a real player, he wasn't chosen—partly because of his questionable athletic skills, but most importantly because of his penchant for combing his hair when he was supposed to be guarding a player from the opposing team. Every few minutes, Teddy would reach for the comb protruding from his back pocket. It was like a personal hygiene compulsion. Teddy would raise his left hand in defense while he carefully manicured his blond tresses with his right hand.

It is no secret that one-armed basketball defenders don't fare well when their opponent dribbles past them while they are in mid-stroke for an easy lay-up. And no amount of laughter and derision from the older boys seemed to deter Teddy from his compulsion. So he was exiled Monday through Friday to the Peanut Gallery where he could comb in peace.

There was also one other more subtle, unspoken reason why Teddy wasn't picked to play in the real games. Technically, he wasn't a member of Muskgrove Lane and since it was important to many of the adults in Muskgrove Lane that Teddy and his family knew their place, it was also important to their children. The one exception was Little Jack. As the neighborhood rebel, he stood on more than one occasion as Teddy's sole defender. Although he was smaller in stature than Teddy, he was a fierce competitor on the Court and was known for starting fights that he knew he couldn't win.

Most of the boys in Muskgrove Lane, younger and older, were not inclined to rile up Little Jack because of his volatile nature, but even Little Jack couldn't get Teddy out of the Peanut Gallery. His one vote simply wasn't enough and besides, he didn't really want Teddy playing on his team. On Monday through Friday Teddy couldn't play, he could only watch, but on Saturday, things were different.

On Saturday, Detective Burns played. He was the only father in the neighborhood that was a Saturday regular. While the other fathers cut their grass, fished and golfed, Lloyd Burns played basketball with a bunch of kids. In fact, his wife, Myrtle, on more than one occasion indicated to the Detective that he was nothing more than a big kid himself. Of course, her comments went in one ear and out the other. While Lloyd loved his wife dearly, as far as sports were concerned Myrtle definitely belonged in the Peanut Gallery.

All the kids and teenagers of Muskgrove Lane referred to Detective Lloyd Burns as "Sarge" in deference to his slight limp, the result of a wound he received in Vietnam and for which he received a Purple Heart. In truth, Sarge was admired not so much because he had received a combat medal or was a Police Detective, but because he could dunk the basketball with either hand whenever he felt like it. He designated his trademark dunk as the "Muskgrove Megadunk" or "M and M" for short.

Although he was judicious in its use, he always demonstrated the "M and M" once or twice each Saturday to the squeals and delight of the "Peanut Gallery." On Saturdays, Sarge was also the Team Captain and Referee. More importantly, he always made sure everyone got to play. His authority and skill were unquestioned.

Sometimes Sarge's team would win and sometimes it wouldn't, but to the bewilderment of the older, more talented players, Sarge always chose the same person first to be on his team. He always chose Teddy. The Monday through Friday spectator was always the first one chosen on Saturday by the neighborhood Superstar.

Sarge's only requirement was that Teddy hand over his comb for the duration of the morning's activities. The older boys looked at each other and shook their heads in disgust as Teddy proudly took his place beside Sarge at Center Court. No one ever knew why Sarge always chose Teddy first. Teddy imagined that Sarge saw some hidden talent in him that wasn't apparent to the others, but then Teddy had always had a vivid and overactive imagination.

Sarge was every bit the Field General on Saturday mornings, preferring to pass the ball and set picks for his younger teammates from the Peanut Gallery. And the Monday through Friday All-Stars knew if they got too rambunctious or aggressive with Sarge's teammates, they would end up eating one of his "M and M's." Sarge would bark orders to his charges as if they were on a do or die combat mission.

"Teddy, guard your flank! PJ's moving to your right!"

"Hands up, Joey!"

"Defense team, Defense!"

"Shoot, Susie, Shoot!"

On Saturdays, the bonds of oppression were cut loose and the spirits of the weekday underclass soared. They imagined they were also players. When the lucky shot was rewarded with a swoosh of the net, they could count on a smile and a wink from Sarge.

"Money in the bank," Sarge would reply, giving the one who scored a "high-five."

On Saturdays, Teddy most of all, came alive for a few hours. On that day, he stood in the light and heard the applause and was called by his name. Unfortunately, Saturday only came once a week. There were six other days in between.

Then one Saturday, Teddy began to change.

Everyone had headed toward home except Sarge, Teddy and Little Jack. Sarge decided that the two of them needed some extra help with their free-throw shooting.

"Hey Sarge, Teddy says he's gonna become a Ninja," Little Jack commented as he threw up another errant free-throw.

"That so?"

Sarge gathered up the rebound and passed the ball to Teddy.

"Yeah," chortled Little Jack. "Teddy's done ordered his uniform."

Teddy bounced the basketball two times, and then swished it through the net.

"That so, Teddy?" Sarge queried, throwing the basketball to Little Jack.

Teddy pulled his comb out of his back pocket and began to run it through his hair.

"Yes Sir, Sarge. I'm gonna earn my black belt in Ninja." Sarge leaned back against the pole that held up the backboard. "Teddy, how you gonna do that—become a Ninja?"

Teddy's eyes lit up in a way Sarge had never seen before. His enthusiasm drew in Little Jack as well. It was like Teddy had found something important that he had been looking for and had eluded him until now.

"I ordered me a Ninja black belt training course from the International Ninja Training Academy for two hundred dollars. It took all my savings, but it'll be worth it. And they included the uniform for free!"

"That so?" Sarge grunted.

"Yes Sir."

"After I complete six lessons and send them in to Master Nu, he'll send me my Black Belt and official Certificate of Graduation."

Although Sarge showed little hint of his approval or disapproval of Teddy's venture, his eyes smiled ever so slightly in response to Teddy's excitement.

"Teddy, why do you want to become a Ninja?"

Without hesitation, Teddy revealed his plan.

"The thing about being a Ninja is that they teach you how to be invisible—you know—in a good way. You can sneak around and even though people won't know you're there, you can be on the look-out."

"Look out for what?" Sarge asked.

"Look out for any danger that might come their way so you can rescue them," Teddy replied somewhat impatiently.

"Your identity stays a secret. It's like you're a secret hero helping out people in trouble. Nobody might ever know the good you do, but at least you'll know. I'm gonna be like the invisible protector of Muskgrove Lane."

Sarge looked at Teddy and gave him a smile.

"Well Teddy, all I can tell you is that I'm glad there'll be a Ninja looking out for me in Muskgrove Lane."

That said, he picked up his basketball and began to walk toward home.

Looking over his shoulder, he shouted, "See you boys next Saturday."

* * *

As the years passed, Muskgrove Lane, like all neighborhoods, endured the usual timeworn transformations marked by the end of some things and the beginning of others. Seasons changed places, hairlines receded, and graduations brushed shoulders with first birthday celebrations. Even Jack shed the "Little" from his childhood moniker. On his fifteenth birthday, Little Jack made it clear that henceforth he would be addressed as "Jack." Anyone who referred to him as Little Jack would do so at his or her own peril, which translated into the teenage code of Muskgrove Lane as an "ass whipping." Occasionally adults slipped up and addressed him as Little Jack. When they did, he met their response with a cold stare and a stony silence. Only Teddy who had always been oblivious to neighborhood etiquette and traditions seemed able to get away with calling Jack, "Little Jack."

On a cool autumn afternoon, Sarge spotted Teddy walking in the rain on the shoulder of Highway Eighty-Seven.

Sarge eased his Jeep Cherokee off the highway, rolled down the passenger side window and waited for Teddy. Within several minutes, Teddy peered in through the open window. "Hi, Sarge."

"Hi, Teddy. How 'bout a ride home?"

"Okay. Thanks," Teddy replied easing himself into the back seat.

Lloyd looked at him in the rearview mirror.

"How's things going?"

Teddy didn't respond right away.

"Me and my stepfather ain't getting along too good. Never really have. He don't understand me. Guess it's hard to understand someone you don't much like."

Teddy's eyes met Lloyd's in the rearview mirror, then he looked out into the rain.

"I don't know what's gonna happen."

The Jeep Cherokee came to a stop where the gravel road began that led to the house trailer.

Lloyd put the gearshift lever in park and turned to Teddy.

"Teddy, whatever happens, I want you to remember something."

"Remember what, Sarge?"

"That you're a good boy."

"You really think so?"

"I know so, Teddy," Lloyd replied.

The corners of Teddy's mouth curved in the hint of a weary smile. He didn't quite believe what Sarge said, but appreciated the gesture nonetheless.

Getting out of the Jeep, Teddy closed the door and peered through the passenger window.

"Thanks for the ride, Sarge."

"Anytime, Teddy."

Lloyd listened to the gravel crunch grinding beneath his wheels as he pulled away from Teddy. He turned his head to look back. He could, just for a moment, barely make out Teddy, climbing his driveway with the heavy uncertain feet of an old man.

* * *

Time moved on. Like most people, the residents of Muskgrove Lane were preoccupied with the busyness of their lives—births, funerals, weddings, graduations and everything that went on in between. Jack and the others graduated from high school and then went off to college, work, or wherever else their dreams and fears led them. The basketball court in the cul-de-sac looked lonely, having to settle for sporadic contests of "Horse" or "Twenty-One." The glory days were gone and like all holiday seasons, Detective Lloyd Burns was overworked and underpaid.

Staring out of his office window and finishing the last of his stale, lukewarm cup of coffee, Lloyd watched the snowflakes float by in the dusk of evening. For police officers and detectives, Christmas wasn't particularly merry. When the phone rang at the precinct station, it wasn't to announce that Santa was passing out gifts, but more likely that he was passed out in an alleyway downtown. For the men and women of Precinct Forty-Four, Christmas was a time of drunken domestic squabbles, traffic accidents initiated by harried, preoccupied last-minute shoppers, and barroom brawls where patrons, not reindeer, sported red noses. Lloyd chuckled softly to himself.

"'Tis the season to be jolly."

"Hey, Lloyd, Officer Klein wants to see you down at Intake," bellowed McGillicutty, the burly Desk Sergeant.

"What does she want?"

McGillicutty looked up from the mound of paperwork on his desk and scowled.

"Hell if I know. What do I look like, a damn encyclopedia!" Lloyd Burns looked at the clock. Ten minutes to quitting time. He grabbed his briefcase and ambled down the hall to the Intake room where he found Patrol Officer Susan Klein thumbing through a dog-eared card file.

"Susan, what can I do for you this fine evening?"

"Probably nothing. I thought I'd give you a head's up on a young guy we just picked up on a solicitation and drug possession charge down in the 'fresh meat' district. Said he knew you." Lloyd's heart sank.

"What's his name?"

Officer Klein flipped through the paperwork on her desk

"Let's see—here it is. He goes by the name Teddy Runion." Lloyd took a deep breath.

"Yeah, I know him. What's the deal on him?"

Scrutinizing her report, Officer Klein talked as she read.

"Looks like it's his third arrest. Twice for prostitution and once for drugs. He's currently on probation which more than likely will be revoked, and since he's just turned eighteen, he may buy some time." Rubbing his chin, Lloyd stared at Officer Klein.

"How 'bout diversion programs? Teddy was a good kid. Grew up in my neighborhood. He had a tough life—not many breaks."

"Yeah, didn't they all," Klein said as she neatly stacked the arrest reports.

"You might try Chris Smith's half-way house over in Chillicowee. He runs a good program. Better than most. A lot of his kids seem to make it."

"Thanks, Klein. I'll check it out. And thanks for the heads up."

"Don't mention it."

Lloyd called his wife as he had done so often before and begged off the Christmas party at her sister's. Having been a police officer's wife for twenty years she understood, but still found it difficult to mask her disappointment. Although he wasn't sure why,

Lloyd didn't tell her about Teddy. There would be time enough for that later.

Lloyd spent the next two and a half hours making calls. Two programs turned him down and a third put Teddy's name on a waiting list. Finally, Chris Smith returned his call. Mustering up the last of his day's energy and stopping just short of begging, Lloyd gave Chris his best shot.

There was a long pause on the other end of the line.

"Okay, Detective. It must be the Christmas spirit. I'll find a way to make room for him. Bring him by tomorrow morning."

"Thanks, Chris. I owe you."

"Yes, you do Detective. Yes, you do."

The good news seemed to refresh Lloyd as he sauntered back down to Intake. He allowed himself a small smile and imagined that this could be the life-changing break that Teddy needed.

Lloyd looked through the interview window at Teddy. He had changed. His blond hair was still meticulously combed, but his face had a drawn, gaunt look to it. His left arm sported a tattoo of an angel.

Lloyd opened the door and walked inside.

"Sarge!" Teddy exclaimed, standing up and extending his hand.

"Hi, Teddy. Long time no see."

Teddy rubbed one eye and kept the other fixated on the badge clinging to Lloyd's coat pocket. "It really has been," he said, nodding to intensify his delivery. "Been a long while. How you doing?"

Teddy stopped rubbing his eye and smiled.

"I've had better days—worse ones too."

Lloyd nodded to an invisible beat and tapped on his coffee cup, his mind scrambling for words.

"Teddy, you know you don't have to live like this. I have friends who could find you a place at a half-way house. There are drug treatment center options, counseling—anything you need." Teddy's face softened, his eyes a little less shaded.

"Sarge, I really appreciate you trying to help me," he said, "but the truth is, I don't want to change." Lloyd leaned in closer.

"You sure? 'Cause I really want . . . I really do know some folks who can help you."

Teddy's face looked older, lines and creases sculpted by long walks up a gravel driveway.

"Yeah, Sarge," he said, "I'm sure."

Lloyd Burns tried, but couldn't hide his distress. He felt like he had been punctured with a giant pin and all the air had been sucked out of him. He tried to give Teddy a smile, but only partially succeeded so instead, he patted him on the shoulder and motioned to Officer Klein that he was through. As she led Teddy out of the office, he turned and looked at the Detective.

"Hey Sarge, you remember that time you gave me a ride home in the rain?"

Lloyd looked up and nodded his head.

"You said I was a good boy. I've never forgotten that."

Sitting in silence, Lloyd cradled his coffee cup in his palm and watched Teddy disappear down the hallway.

8

Hold the Line

MICHAEL BRASWELL

THE SWELTERING HEAT SEEMED TO SUCK THE OXYGEN OUT OF THE small, dilapidated shack where the two GI's were holed up. Ray lit another cigarette off Morgan's. "You see any movement out there?"

Morgan took off his helmet and wiped the sweat from his brow. "Not since we took care of that recon patrol this morning. 'Course, who knows when they'll send another one? How's our ammo holding out?"

"We're down to two grenades," Ray replied. "We're ok with the machine guns."

Morgan peered through the binoculars at the hedgerow and tree line. "Whatever it takes, we've got to hold the line."

He tossed his cigarette butt on the floor of the shack and ground it out with his boot. "These Winstons are ok, but I like the taste of the Menthols better."

Ray blew a smoke ring. "Yeah, me too. What kind of rations we got left?"

Rummaging through his field pack, Morgan handed Ray a canteen. "Looks pretty good. Two canteens full of grape Kool-Ade, one pimento cheese sandwich, one peanut butter and jelly and four graham crackers. We ate the sardines yesterday. You want peanut butter and jelly or pimento cheese?"

Ray flipped the remains of his cigarette out of the window as he quickly scanned the tree line for any sign of enemy activity. "How about pimento cheese? I had peanut butter and jelly for supper last night."

Morgan handed his friend a sandwich. "One pimento cheese coming up."

The field rations menu for sixth grade warriors was limited. The two boys washed down their rations with grape Kool-Ade and tap water. Ray stretched and yawned. "I tried to snatch some menthols from my Mother's stash, but she was out so I had sneak a pack from my Dad's carton of Winston's."

Tapping a cigarette against the pack like they do in the movies, Morgan wedged it behind his ear and looked out the window. "Sometimes you have to make do with what you can get. By the way, my Mom's coming to pick me up around five o'clock."

"Five!" Ray exclaimed. "I thought you'd be spending the night. Don't you remember our plan for our nighttime raid? I even got face paint."

Morgan took the cigarette from behind his ear and lit it. "I know, I know. Trouble is, my Mom outranks me. I'll be tied up every evening this week."

"Doing what?" Ray queried fishing another Winston out of the pack.

"Vacation Bible School."

Ray fumbled with the matches. "All week?"

"Yep," Morgan replied. "All week."

Slinging his helmet to the floor, Ray shrugged in exasperation. "Well, hell, it is what it is. I guess we'll have to postpone night maneuvers until next week."

"Guess so," Morgan said as he drained the last of the Kool-Ade from his canteen and smacked his lips.

Ray kicked his field pack. "Wait a minute! Next week my Dad has to go for his appointment at the Veteran's hospital."

Morgan perked up. "You never told me your Daddy was a veteran. What was he—army, navy, marines?"

"Air Force. He was a fighter pilot in Europe. Flew a P-51 Mustang," Ray replied softly.

"Fighter pilot! Hot damn, a fighter pilot. I can't believe you never told me he was a fighter pilot. And he flew a P-51 Mustang— king of the skies!"

Morgan looked like he was ready to dance a jig. "I just finished reading a library book about German fighter pilots. I bet your Daddy has some tales to tell. How many Messerschmitt 109s and Fock-Wulfes did he shoot down?"

"I don't know."

"You don't know?" Morgan continued. "I can't believe you don't know that. Well, we'll just have to ask him."

Ray looked at his hands. "We can't."

Morgan looked at his friend incredulously. "Why the hell not?"

"Because I'm not supposed to know," Ray replied quietly. "Since you're my best friend, I'll tell you why as long as you promise not to tell anyone else."

Ray grabbed Morgan's wrist and looked at him with all the solemnity a boy his age could muster. "It's a promise that can't be broken."

Nodding his head to the affirmative, Morgan and Ray sat on their backpacks and lit two fresh cigarettes.

Finally, Ray spoke. "My Mom told me about it so I could understand why my Dad acts the way he does. I'm glad she told me because before she did, it could get pretty scary. Two or three times a week my Dad wakes up in the middle of the night. Sometimes I can hear him hollering—one time I heard him scream like some wild animal. Then things quiet down. Once I sneaked down the hall and I could hear him crying and my Mom whispering to him like she does to me when I have a nightmare. When he wakes up like that, he doesn't go back to sleep. I can hear him walking back and forth on our back porch until the sun comes up. Sometimes, when things get really bad, he goes to the Veterans hospital for a couple of weeks."

Ray paused and turned his head for a moment. "Just a minute, I got something in my eye."

Morgan offered him a cigarette.

Waving off the cigarette, Ray looked at his friend somberly. "My Dad's squadron fire-bombed Dresden. When he dropped napalm from his plane, he saw women and children running down the street on fire. My Mom said he's never been the same since. The time he woke up screaming, I was worried and tiptoed to their bedroom to see if everything was all right. I stood outside the door and heard my Dad tell my Mom he wished he had died in that fire."

The two friends embraced the silence Ray's testimony demanded.

Ray picked up his army surplus helmet and brushed some dried mud off of it. "My Dad doesn't even want me to play army. Says he heard about plenty of German boy soldiers no older than me who were killed in the fighting."

Morgan reached over and gently patted his friend on the back. "War can sure be a bitch."

"I guess so," Ray muttered as he stared at the floor.

A car horn sounded like a trumpet, displacing the melancholy the two boys shared. Morgan heard his mother calling for him.

Picking up his gear, he turned to Ray. "Maybe we both need a little R and R."

Ray smiled at Morgan. "Vacation Bible School doesn't sound much like R and R to me."

"Better me than you," Morgan hollered as he ran toward his mother's station wagon. "Rest up. Week after next we'll plan a major offensive."

9

Three Summers

MICHAEL BRASWELL

SCHOOL WAS OUT AND SUMMER WAS IN FULL SWING. THE SOUTH Georgia heat and humidity signaled that swarms of gnats and mosquitoes were waking up from their winter naps to begin the season's torment of young and old alike.

I was gearing up for my usual summer routine—mowing yards, playing baseball and fantasizing about girls. Fourteen was an in-between age for me and my buddies. We liked what we saw and knew what we wanted, but riding three speed Schwinns caused our fantasies to come up two years short. Sixteen meant a driver's license and the possibility of riding on four wheels instead of two. Sixteen meant that what we dreamed about might be within our reach.

After Sunday dinner, my father turned my routine plans into chaos with the words, "I got you a job at the Coca-Cola bottling plant. You start tomorrow at seven sharp." No negotiation. End of story. Seven A.M. to five P.M., Monday through Friday. The pay?

One dollar an hour, including overtime when required. Oh yes, I could mow yards on Saturdays, my day off. Case closed.

On the first day, Columbus Evans, the plant manager and part-time minister, introduced me to the all-important Time Clock and Ernestine, the office secretary who wore her bouffant hairdo like a Queen wore her crown. From there it was straight to the production floor for my fifteen-minute orientation.

The production process was straightforward enough. Dirty bottles in and the finished products—Coca-Cola, Fanta Orange, Fresca and Tab—out. The hardest jobs were at the beginning of the process where the dirty work was done. Not the showroom out front with the big, well-lit picture windows where folks walking by could see the pretty, clean bottles full of Coke moving along the conveyor belt destined for country stores, cafes and home refrigerators. No, the dirty work occurred in the back, out of sight where it belonged.

Two crates at a time, holding twenty-four empty bottles on a worktable, placing them upright on a moving steel mesh belt, which moved the dirty bottles into slots, which then carried them through the cleaning and washing phase of the process. The term "dirty" carried a special meaning regarding soda bottles. Empty bottles held a variety of contents and residue, including the urine of small children whose fathers didn't want to stop for a bathroom break on the way to Grandma's, cigarette and cigar butts, and the occasional dead mouse, leech or insect. The hapless soul assigned to "racking bottles" had to keep the conveyor belt full and the bottles upright while playing dodge ball with unintended spills. Multi-tasking such as it was, required one to do a kind of a dance, stacking the crates on the work table, racking twenty-four piss-filled bottles at a time and placing them intact on a moving conveyor belt. Needless to say, this was not a job for the faint-hearted. Mercifully, frequent mechanical breakdowns gave the one tasked with this job a brief respite, a chance to step into the adjoining alleyway in hopes of catching the flutter of a rogue summer breeze while wiping one's brow with the tail of his sweat-stained T-shirt.

Once cleaned, the bottles continued their journey on another conveyor belt to be refilled with "the taste that refreshes." On the final leg of the bottling process they passed in formation by a light designed to reveal any imperfections that might make them unfit for the lips of thirsty consumers. On occasion as mentioned previously, a cigarette butt or two or a dead mouse or bug were spotted whereby the bottle in question was quickly removed from the moving parade of freshly minted sodas. One might assume that sitting on a stool and watching bottles full of Coca-Cola pass by was the easiest of the jobs available in a bottling plant. It was and it wasn't. While there were no physical demands placed on the quality control sentry, the concentration required for closely observing the moving line of bottles filled with soda was in fact, quite demanding. Nodding off was the primary enemy of the watchful eye, seducing the hapless observer with the hypnotic effects of moving objects against the backdrop of a warm, soothing light. Big John almost got fired for falling asleep twice on one four-hour shift of "light duty."

The refurbished sodas reached their final destination when they fell twenty-four at a time, into waiting crates which once filled, rolled down yet another conveyor belt where they were stacked six rows high, thirty cases to a pallet. The forklift operator then moved them to the warehouse where they were stacked in rows six pallets high.

My first job was keeping the piece of equipment through which refilled bottles dropped into the waiting crates twenty-four at a time, unjammed and at the same time, stacking the crates on a wooden pallet which would be moved in an orderly fashion into the adjoining warehouse. Although on the back end of the production process, it proved to be an arduous task. I did my best. Clarence and Big John, two black workers, tried to help out when they could, but the piece of equipment I was responsible for continued to jam. Thirty minutes into my first big summer job, I heard Monroe Herman, a maintenance mechanic, utter the fateful words, "You're fired. Get your things and go home."

Having never been fired, it was an embarrassing moment. Of course, I had never worked for anyone except the folks I mowed yards for and my father, who on occasion, had lit a fire in me of another kind. Stunned by Herman's verdict, it took me a few moments to process the consequences as Clarence and Big John looked on. Not sure what to do next, I returned to the plant office to clock out one hour after I had clocked in. Columbus Evans looked up from his paperwork and said, "What are you doing, son?" Shrugging my shoulders, I replied that I had been fired by the maintenance mechanic. Frowning, the plant manager shook his head. "Herman can't fire you or anybody else. Get back to work." So, I did. I learned later that summer from Clarence why Monroe Herman was so ornery. Several years earlier during the holidays, he was on the roof of his house repairing his chimney. Unknown to him, his three-year-old grandson had crawled into the empty hearth. Monroe accidentally dropped a brick down the chimney, killing his grandson. His deep wound of sorrow hid behind his perpetual scowl. Who could hold hard feelings toward a man who had gone through that? Certainly, not me.

By the end of June, I had graduated to working the "rack" with the occasional stint of "light duty." The apron I wore while racking dirty bottles caught most, but not all of the bodily fluids and other debris spilling from overturned bottles. The one advantage in doing that particular job was that time passed quickly. One had to hustle and maintain good eye-hand coordination to work the "rack." Twelve o'clock came before you knew it. Time for lunch. Clarence, Big John and I usually walked the seven blocks to downtown where we would part company for the duration of the lunch hour, me to "The Gold Leaf" restaurant to join my father and the two of them to the "Blue Moon Cafe" in the black section of town. On one such occasion, Clarence taught me one of life's important lessons.

It was 1962, my second summer at the bottling plant. Frank Sinatra couldn't have been referring to 1962 when he crooned "It was a very good year." It was a time when the Civil Rights movement was gaining steam and racial tensions were in the air. Although integration laws had been passed, restaurants like The Gold Leaf were posting signs in their windows and placing placards on their tables stating things like "We reserve the right to refuse service to customers." Baptist churches were drawing up contingency plans on how to respond to Blacks who tried to attend Sunday morning services. After much prayer and deliberation, their heaven-sent conclusion was to have ushers escort them out of the sanctuary if they tried to enter—by force, if necessary. There were other rumblings and whispers in that year as well. Groups like the Klu Klux Klan and the John Birch Society wondered if the time was finally ripe, if it was safe for them to come out of the shadows where they had been lurking.

It was during such a time that Clarence and I walked toward town during our lunch hour. As we walked, he turned to me and asked, "Do you consider me your friend—that I should have the same rights as you?"

"Of course, I do," I quickly replied. And like young teenage boys are prone to do, I puffed up a bit and continued with something like, "And if anyone says anything different, I'd tell them that they are full of crap."

Clarence turned to me and calmly said, "Then you won't mind if I join you and your father for lunch at the Gold Leaf."

More than sixty years later, I can still remember my visceral reaction. I broke out in a cold sweat, my knees buckled and I didn't know what to say. Walking down the sidewalk, we were only four store-fronts from the Gold Leaf. My bluff had been called. The high and mighty limb I was perched on had been sawed off. I was in emotional free-fall. Armageddon was waiting on me two store-fronts down.

Finally, I coughed out, "Well, if you really want to. . ."

Clarence waited until I stopped in front of the Gold Leaf. He laughed and said, "See you after lunch."

My summer education continued as I became more skilled with bottling room tasks. I listened and watched. I listened as Big John and Clarence talked about their second jobs cleaning downtown stores at night after work. About how they lived for Saturday nights, getting their party clothes from the cleaners, shining their shoes to a high shine and drinking scotch whiskey mixed with sweet milk. I also learned about sex. That if a man spent the night with a woman named Flovilla, he better bring his toothbrush. And how a lecherous, old local lawyer liked to visit the Black side of town in search of sexual favors before attending church with his wife on Sunday morning. I learned how to wrestle hundred pound sacks of sugar onto stacks in the plant's attic and hide out with Clarence and Big John for a rest break before the next work assignment.

Near the end of my second summer's stint with Coca Cola bottling, I graduated to fork-lift operator, the crème de la crème of jobs. It was like getting my driver's license early. Stacking thirty case pallets on top of each other six rows high with a fork-lift was a plum assignment in the bottling world. Wheeling around the plant, speeding from one section to another was what dreams were made of. And on rainy days when production shut down for scheduled maintenance and the boss wasn't around, Big John and I would race our fork-lifts with wild abandon, making U turns and dodging rows of soft drinks. For a fifteen-year-old, it was almost like being a jet pilot. But there was a downside. His name was Alvin Lightler.

Alvin Lightler was twenty-one, six years older than me. He had worked at the bottling plant since he was eighteen. Alvin was twice my size and well-muscled. Unfortunately, he was also well-muscled where his brain was supposed to be located. Roscoe, the chief maintenance engineer, referred to him as Alvin "Lights-out." When his name came up around Big John, his response was simply, "dumbass." Alvin had made it known on more than one occasion that he wanted to drive a fork-lift. He wasn't fast or dexterous enough to handle the Rack and he was tired of stacking pallets of bottled sodas all day long. Needless to say, Alvin didn't take kindly to me, a mere teenage rookie, being promoted to fork-lift operator ahead of him. He was mightily pissed. I could see it in his eyes. Then one day it happened.

I had been sent to a remote area of the warehouse to retrieve a clipboard when Alvin stepped out from behind a drink machine and confronted me. As he was apt to do, he got right to the point. "I'm gonna whip your ass." And I had no doubt that he could. Just as he reared his fist back to take his pound of flesh from the person he imagined had stolen his forklift opportunity, a massive black hand took hold of his collarbone. Picking him up like a child and setting him aside, Big John looked Alvin in the eye and said matter-of-factly, "Don't be messin' with my boy."

My last summer started off with a bang when I ditched the Schwinn for a 1959 Chevy Bel Air. The two-door coupe had a six-cylinder engine with a three-speed stick shift on the column. It sported a two-tone white and somewhere between pink and purple—I preferred purple—paint job with something that looked like wings on the rear end. It wasn't the Ford T-Bird I dreamed about, but it was a car, the bridge from my active imagination to the pursuit of whatever caught my fancy. Me and my buddies could join the Saturday night parade, circling the local Dairy Queen with a dozen other cars before pooling our money for burgers and fries. We could head off to the local youth center to check out the girls, talking big and trying to muster up the courage to ask one out. A car pointed toward the possibility of a date, maybe even a drive-in date where anything could happen.

The summer of 1963 only got better from there. Much to my surprise, the owner of Coca-Cola bottling decided he wanted to give his eighteen-year-old bound for college son a taste of real work—not too hard, but hard enough. Lucky me caught the assignment. No more stacking and racking. Me and Junior headed for the open road in our official Coca-Cola pick-up truck. From Funston to Cool Springs, we delivered and picked up drink machines throughout the county. We also tried our hand at making and delivering signs that were to be mounted on country store rooftops.

I didn't forget about Clarence and Big John. We still stacked bags of sugar and raced forklifts when the opportunity presented itself. And having my own set of wheels allowed me to spend occasional Friday nights shooting pool with Clarence at the "Harlem Two-Spot" in the black section of town. On the first night of weekend camping trips when me, Rob, Bert and Jimmy Mack were making our final run for provisions, we would pull up to the "Higher Ground Funeral Home" in my faithful Chevy to purchase a half-pint of Vodka from Big John who functioned as the middle man for us under-age drinkers. He brought it out to the car and often said, "You boys be careful." He handed me the half-pint and I handed him a five-dollar bill. In those days, a half-pint of Vodka was all it took to fuel the tall tales and wild fantasies of four teenage boys on a two-night camping foray into the woods. Hot dogs, chips, Seven-Ups and a half-pint around a campfire provided the makings of a weekend of magic.

As good as that summer was, like all good things, it came to an end. Its conclusion proved bittersweet. I came to understand that Clarence and Big John had worked at the bottling plant for three years and still earned the same pay as me, one dollar an hour. Me, Alvin, Big John and Clarence were all paid the same while everyone else had earned raises of one sort or another. I could understand why as a summer worker, me and Alvin for obvious reasons, were paid the same, but Big John and especially Clarence, who was as smart as anybody in the bottling room, deserved more. It didn't set well with them and I began to hear mutterings about them leaving town and going to Chicago where Clarence's cousin lived, to get better jobs. And that's what they did. I found out in the fall that they were gone. Although I was happy for them, I knew I would miss them. As for spending my summers mowing grass and playing baseball (which I wasn't very good at anyway), that was a distant memory three years past. The silver lining was that I had saved a goodly sum of money, just enough to purchase an electric guitar and an Amp. With three other friends, we formed a local rock and roll band, "The Undertakers," which enjoyed the long run all of twelve months playing here and there. We weren't all that good, but we had fun and thought for one moment in a state of collective delirium that we might just be the next "Rolling Stones."

10

House of the Rising Sun

ANTHONY CAVENDER

BRIGHT NIGHTS. BIG CITY. IN 1966 ON A SULTRY FRIDAY NIGHT, the visit to the brothel began with a dare. We were cruising around East Nashville in my mint green 1963 Chevrolet Impala, a 283 with three on a tree. Making the usual tour, we checked out car hop restaurants, popular drag racing streets, Shelby Park where young studs displayed their rides and shot the shit, and of course, drove by the houses of several good-looking girls in the hope of catching a glimpse or better yet, striking up a conversation with one of them. We talked about many things, such as what college was going to be like. Mike ("Parrot") Graham and Rob ("Britches") Blann would be attending Vanderbilt, Bill ("Skull") Carpenter was headed for Martin Methodist College, and I ("Red Snapper") was going to Belmont College. We also talked about the possibility of going to Vietnam because we were not sure if the "4F" college deferment in the draft would hold out. Should we go ahead and sign up for one of the armed forces that would less likely send us into the rice patties and jungles, like the Navy and Air Force? Skull pointed out that this maneuver would entail four years of service, but that the two additional years would be better than dying. Most of our conversation, however, was devoted to girls. We were obsessed with girls. In fact, the primary purpose of cruising was to meet girls. We frequently discussed the mysteries of the female body and what we would do if we ever found ourselves intimate with one. We had all made it to "second base" with a girl, but none of us had hit the home run. In the Department of Love, we were all rookies. We practiced on ourselves what we wanted to do with real girls, not the fantasies we found in Playboy magazines and Sears and Roebuck catalog lingerie sections. We were, as Dylan Thomas put it, "wild boys, innocent as strawberries," and on this night, as with every other night of cruising, we were salmon swimming upstream.

We were sitting in my car eating cheeseburgers when Parrot brought up the idea of going to a brothel to dispose of our boyhood innocence. A classmate, Jimmy Pierce, had recently told him about a place called "Good Jellies" in North Nashville.

"That's a poor, black area," Skull said. "I don't think it would be smart for four white boys to go there."

None of us had much contact with black people during those days. Our neighborhoods were solidly white and middle class. Nashville had installed a school integration program our senior year, but the few black students bused to our high school, Stratford, were in the lower grades. I don't think any of us had a black friend, except maybe for Britches when he attended integrated schools on US Army bases. Our reticence for venturing into North Nashville rested partly on our ignorance of black society, which was plentiful, and stereotypes. For us, venturing into North Nashville was in some ways tantamount to going on an expedition into the uncharted jungles of the Congo. That's how naïve we were. Our reluctance, however, derived more from a kind of primal fear of meeting folks who possessed justifiable feelings of anger and violence born of two hundred years of brutal oppression by our people, white people.

"It'll be okay, man," Parrot said. "We'll have each other's back. I've heard that a lot of white guys go there. Anyway, where's your sense of adventure?"

"Yeah, well, who wants to get syphilis?" I asked.

"Use a condom, dumbass!" Parrot said.

"And what if the condom tears? They aren't fail-safe, dumbass."

"And what if a bat flies out of my ass right now and shits on your head?"

"And what if you kiss my ass?"

"I would, but you don't have one."

"Look, I'd be willing to go there with you, but I'm not interested in screwing a whore." Skull and Britches nodded their heads in agreement.

Britches, who was wired from soaking up four cups of coffee in two hours, leaned across the front seat toward Parrot. "How about YOU screw a whore and then tell us what it's like? I dare you to do it! We can all chip in and cover the cost. What do you think?"

"Hold on," Skull chirped in. "How much is this gonna cost?"

We pulled out all the money we had, which amounted to $26.00, and concluded that would probably be enough.

"So, Parrot, are you in or are you out?" Britches asked.

"Hell, yeah! But you chicken shits have to go with me." We all agreed to go both to serve as witnesses to such a momentous event, a rite of passage, and if necessary, to provide protection. But to a man, we were mostly curious about what a brothel was like. None of us really believed Parrot would go through with it and none of us would have blamed him if he didn't.

A high pressure system had settled over the Nashville basin, effectively sealing in the pollution, humidity, and heat which created a ghostly haze that hung lazily over the city. All the windows in the car were rolled down as we headed down Gallatin Road toward downtown and the Jefferson Street Bridge. We sang along with Levi Stubbs and the Four Tops's hit, "Sugar Pie Honey Bunch" on the radio, and after it finished, we revisited our long-standing argument as to who's the better band: the Beatles or the Rolling Stones. Parrot, who loved the Stones and was inclined to hyperbole, maintained that "Satisfaction" was the greatest rock and roll song of all time. I agreed with him, and still do to this day. And then "Ballad of the Green Berets" came on the radio.

"Change the station," I said.

"They're selling the fucking war, man, and I'm not buying," Parrot said.

"Fuck the Green Berets," Britches added. "What are we doing in Vietnam anyway? Stopping the spread of communism? Is that it? Gimme a break."

"Think about this: We go to Vietnam and get our asses blown off and we never got laid," Parrot said. "That would be tragic."

We crossed the bridge and made our way down Jefferson Street, passing Charlie Nickens's Barbeque Restaurant. I had eaten there several times with my parents after church on Sundays. We usually ordered the pulled barbeque pork on a corn cake topped with a pickle. I remember how the obsequious behavior of the waiters, all of them black, made me feel uncomfortable. I had only ventured past Charlie Nickens's once when we drove to the house where my mother's parents lived, a few blocks off Jefferson Street in a neighborhood known as Kalb (pronounced as "cab") Hollow, which was adjacent to another neighborhood, Germantown. They ran a boarding house and my grandfather, who was affectionately known as "the mayor of Kalb Hollow," worked in a foundry and as a saloon keeper. Over the years, my mother's kin along with many whites in North Nashville moved ("fled" would be a more accurate word) across the Cumberland River into East Nashville as North Nashville became predominately black.

The directions given to us by Jimmy Pierce were vague. All we had to go on was a street name and that Good Jellies could be identified by a blue light on the porch. As we entered into no-man's-land Skull asked, "What happened to the red light?" Parrot chimed in that it should be green for "go, baby, go!" So we drove slowly and aimlessly through neighborhoods with unknown boundaries and streets lined with dilapidated cracker box and shotgun houses, many of them built in the late 1800s. The summer haze was thick and the air fouled from the smoke of smoldering dumpster fires that slowly burned night and day. It was pushing 10:00 and eighty degrees, but there was a lot of activity: men working on cars propped up on jack stands and concrete blocks, radios blaring, people out on their front porches seeking refuge from the heat and carrying on conversations with neighbors next door, on the sidewalks, or across the street. There were also a few drunks tottering along with a bottle of Colt 45 or Mad Dog 20/20 in a bag. Skinny street dogs ran about looking for food. At one point we had to stop the car when we encountered two men fighting in the middle of the street. It was savage. One guy knocked the other guy to the ground and then sat on top of him, hitting him in the face again and again until someone finally broke it up. Add a continuous acid rain drizzle and huge neon billboards and you'd have the movie set of *Blade Runner*.

These sights and sounds were not unfamiliar to us. There were such neighborhoods in East Nashville, like the infamous high crime Fatherland Street area. The only difference was this one was occupied by poor blacks and the other by poor whites. From our perspective, all the poor neighborhoods of Nashville were war zones to be avoided. There were, of course, sedate, safe, black neighborhoods with well-kept houses and lawns in North Nashville, but we were unaware of them.

We finally found the street we were looking for and drove back and forth looking for the infamous blue light, all the while feeling dangerously conspicuous and frightened. Finally, Britches suggested that we abandon our quest when we passed by an old man standing alone on a street corner. Parrot abruptly grabbed my arm and shouted "stop the car!" "Let's ask him where Good Jellies is." "No, man, let's get the hell out of here," Skull replied. Against my better judgment, I put the car in reverse and backed up.

"Excuse me, sir," Parrot said. "We're looking for Good Jellies. Can you tell us where to find it?"

He was a scarecrow of a man, with scraggly beard specked with grey, rheumy eyes, and a stooped frame. The old man's baggy pants were held up by red suspenders. His bald head was topped with a frayed straw hat. He gave us a hard look that we couldn't fathom before saying, "Miss Good Jellies been dead a long time." Then he broke into a smile. "If you boys is lookin' for a poke, you can go right down the street here to Miss Nadine's, fourth house on the right. Umm-hum." "Poke"? We had never heard the word used this way, but its meaning was abundantly clear. The old man asked if we could spare some change for a beer. We thanked him for his help, gave him fifty cents and headed toward Nadine's.

After parking the car in front of Nadine's, we debated whether we should leave or stay. All the while, a woman, whom we assumed was the Madame, Nadine, swayed back and forth on a porch swing fanning herself and starring a hole through us. Throwing up his hands in frustration, Britches said, "Go check it out, Parrot. You're the reason we're here." We sat in silence watching him talk with the woman, and then he gestured for us to get out of the car.

Our hands in our pockets, we stood nervously on the front porch as Parrot introduced us. "Boys," he said, "this here is Nadine." Almost in unison, we chortled, "Nice to meet you, Ma'am."

Nadine looked to be around fifty years old and was anything but pretty. She had extremely large breasts that sagged down to her waist and stubby arms and legs. "You boys wait here for a moment," Nadine said, and then went into the house.

Britches looked at Parrot, then at the rest of us. "So, you're going through with this?"

"It depends."

"Depends on what?" I asked.

"On what the prostitute looks like. I'm not getting down with someone who looks like Nadine!"

"Can't say as I blame you," Skull said, laughing.

"Nadine said she could hook us up with a younger girl, someone around our age. Let's see what happens."

"So, did you asked her how much it cost?" Britches asked, pulling the dollar bills out of his blue jeans' pocket.

"Twenty bucks."

"Good deal," Britches replied with enthusiasm, "you're covered!"

"Did it happen to occur to you all," I asked, "that this might be a set-up for getting rolled or worse?"

We were frozen in the thought of that possibility when Nadine reappeared and took a seat on the porch swing. She told us to go on into the parlor and have a seat. "June-Bug will be with you shortly."

We did as she instructed. The parlor was small. A couch with a faded green and yellow afghan draped on it took up much of the space. There was a bird cage with no bird. A radiant Jesus standing on top of a mountain with his arms unfurled looked down from a picture hanging on a wall as if to say, "What are you boys doing here?" A hallway that led to the back of the house had no door but instead, a beaded curtain. Next to the doorway was a record player on a roller stand. We all scrunched together on the couch.

Suddenly, June-Bug emerged through the beaded curtain wearing a beige negligee that fell just below her butt. Much to our surprise, she was a very attractive young woman in her early twenties with a slim body and firm breasts. Her hair was done in the emerging Afro style. She smiled at us as she put a 45 on the turntable. The record cranked out "Hold On, I'm Comin'" by Sam and Dave. The double entendre was not lost on us. She didn't do a belly dance, but I couldn't help but think of Little Egypt. Her dance routine included moves from some of the popular dances of the day we had all watched on American Band Stand, the Jerk, the Swim, and the Pony. Although none of her moves were overtly sexual, if the circumstances had been different, there's no doubt we all would have been sporting a boner.

About halfway through the song she abruptly stopped dancing, clumsily lifted the stylus off the record causing a zip sound, smiled at us and said, "Which of you young men want to be with me tonight?" As Parrot got up from the couch, Britches slipped him our collection of twenty dollars. June-Bug took his hand and led him through the beaded curtain. The rest of us sat anxiously on the couch in wait for his return.

Curiosity eventually got the best of me. I slid off the couch and stuck my head through the beaded curtain. I was momentarily stunned when I saw in a dimly lit room, a tall, large man reclined on a bed with an arm resting across his eyes. He had stripped down to his shorts and tee shirt to cool down. A wine bottle was on the floor next to the bed. He didn't move a muscle, yet he knew I was there. "Ain't nobody 'lowed back here without Miss Nadine or one of the girls." "Yes, sir," I said sheepishly, and quickly returned to the couch.

Ten minutes had passed when Parrot finally returned to the parlor with June-Bug. "So, how did it go?" Skull asked. "I couldn't do it," he replied meekly, looking down at the floor. None of us were crushed by this admission. In fact, we were all relieved. June-Bug looked at us sitting on the couch. "Any of you interested? How 'bout you?" she said, looking directly at me. "No, thanks." And then to Skull, "You?" "No Ma'am." And then to Britches, "You?" "No thanks." Then June-Bug matter-of-factly said, "You boys need to hit the road if you ain't interested. You know what I'm sayin'?" We knew what she was saying and went out the door. As we stepped off the porch, Miss Nadine smiled at us. "You boys come back, now."

As soon as we got in the car we pelted Parrot with questions about why he backed out. He looked out of his passenger window before replying, "Man, it just didn't feel right."

Apparently, there was a couple in a room next door and the moans and groans of them going at it spooked him. Plus, the sheets were soiled and dirty. A long silence followed that Britches broke by asking Parrot what he and June-Bug had done for the ten minutes they were together. "Did she jerk you off? Did she blow you? What?"

"No, none of that," Parrot replied. "We just talked."

Skull looked at the rest of us and rolled his eyes. "Talked? Talked about what?!"

Parrot said nothing and looked straight ahead.

It was around eleven thirty when we started toward home. With a twelve o'clock curfew, the night was winding down although greater Jefferson Street was coming alive. Cars stuffed with raucous people in the mood to party slowly cruised the streets. Music from the jukeboxes and bands in the beer joints flowed into the streets. "High society" night clubs like the Baron, Del Morocco, New Era, and Maceos, where people came dressed to kill, were filling up. Chartbusters like Jerry Butler, Little Richard, Etta James, B.B. King, Ray Charles, Aretha Franklin, and Jimi Hendrix performed in these clubs in the 1950s and '60s, along with local favorites like Ironing Board Sam and Bobby Hebb. In fact, we knew nothing about this hidden world in Nashville even though we listened to a lot of black music on the radio.

At a stop light we found ourselves next to a dazzling Oldsmobile Starfire with four black dudes who were obviously on their way to getting plastered. "Lookie here," one of them said as the other three erupted in laughter." We got four white boys who looks like they be lost!" We averted their gaze and said nothing, expecting to hear them call us "honkies" or "crackers," or maybe even jump us, but, instead, one of them in the backseat leaned out his window with a bottle of wine in his hand and said, "You boys want a drink?" "No thanks," I replied with my dorky white-boy voice an octave too high, "We don't care for wine." "Whaaaaaaaaaaa? Everybody like wine!" The light changed and we sped away.

As we rolled along, taking in the sights and sounds, a more relaxed Parrot related his conversation with June-Bug. He learned that June-Bug was a nickname given to her by Miss Nadine. Her real name was Allison. She was a rising junior at Tennessee State University majoring in elementary education. She came from a poor family of nine kids and worked part-time in a grocery store and as a prostitute to cover tuition and books. Her parents didn't know she was one of Nadine's girls.

As I pulled the car into the driveway of Parrot's house, I politely reminded him to return the money that we had given him to get laid.

"I don't have it," he said.

"What do you mean you don't have it?"

"What I said, I don't have it."

"We heard that you don't have it, dickhead. What happened to our money?"

"I gave it to Allison."

"You what . . . you gave it to the prostitute?" Britches said in astonishment. "Why would you do a dumb-ass thing like that?"

"Because she's a really smart girl and she needs the money for college."

"Man, she could have been bullshitting you," Skull countered.

"Maybe, but I don't think so."

We reconciled ourselves to the loss of the money in recognition of Parrot's act of kindness, stupid or not.

"Hey!" Britches said. "I heard Gwendolyn Brooks is having a party at her house tomorrow night. Let's crash it!"

"Maybe Lynn Lunn will be there," Skull mused. "She's hot as a firecracker!"

I smiled at the thought of it. "I'll pick y'all up at seven sharp."

II

From Whence I Came

DONALD BALL

BEING A CHILD OF THE SOUTH, IT HAS LONG BEEN AN INGRAINED part of my mindset that both my family and its history are integral and inseparable parts of my identity. I have never lost track of the fact that my life is but a small part of a deeply rooted and ever un-folding saga which began long before my birth and will continue into the unforeseeable future. My recollections remind me how their often subtle, but ever-present, influences shape much of how I view the world around me.

Though their home was rich in love and heart, money was another matter for my great-grandfather's struggling household in the countryside of Coffee County. Despite the desire to make their children's Christmas as enjoyable as possible, available resources would only stretch so far in a home with too many children and too little cash.

As a young lady still in her teens, my grandmother's sole present one Christmas prior to World War I was a small carnival glass bowl. While such glassware may be avidly sought after by today's antique collectors, at the time such items were very inexpensive and cost just a few cents each. But to a small girl in the countryside, it was a very special gift of the heart from her parents and was an item to be cherished. Humble though it may have been, it remained in her procession until her death almost seventy years later as a reminder of the love of her parents and the happy days of her childhood.

As a young man in pursuit of bettering himself, my grandfather, Claude Lee McFarland, enrolled on the eve of the Great War for what proved to be his one and only year of college at Middle Tennessee State Normal School (now Middle Tennessee State University) in Murfreesboro. With the entry of the United States into the conflict, the college offered male students with a farm background full credit for any classes in which they were then registered, to go back to the country and bring in the crop as a contribution to the war effort. My grandfather accepted the offer. The credits he earned as a result were sufficient to qualify him for a lifetime teacher's certificate from the State of Tennessee. Shortly after fulfilling his obligation to harvest the crop, he was hired as the teacher for the McMahan School in the ephemeral settlement of the same name in southeastern Cannon County. At that time, this small dot on the map was a community which consisted of a few houses and the schoolhouse situated next to the cemetery. The area has changed little since then except at present there are fewer houses and a newer frame structure housing the McMahan Church of Christ which was built on the site of the old one room school.

Days began early for the students comprising the school's eight grades. One of the first tasks each morning during the cold weather was for the students to forage through the nearby woods for firewood to heat the school. This necessity was due to the local school board's view that expenditures on such things was a frivolous waste of taxpayer's money. They were a frugal bunch, apparently more interested in saving money than in educating their children. Their frugality extended beyond the need for warmth in the learning environment.

Even the most dedicated young scholars attending school occasionally found it necessary to answer the call of nature—except the school board didn't believe in wasting money on building privies either. When needs arose, young ladies were excused and availed themselves of one end of a nearby woodlot while young gentlemen ventured to the other end.

Two years of dealing with a school board unwilling to furnish either firewood or the most rudimentary sanitary facilities—in concert with the dismal pay—prompted my grandfather to seek other avenues of employment. In later years, he recalled with a chuckle the irony that in some instances, he was but a year or two older than some of his students. Indeed, in the early 1980s he received a cheery Christmas card from one of the girls he had taught as her schoolmaster of six decades past. She, like my grandfather, had by that time long been a great-grandparent, yet each recalled a simpler though challenging time from long ago.

My grandfather was the subject of gentle chiding throughout his married life for being a "cheapskate," despite his many acts of generosity to family and friends alike. Though I never knew what prompted the selection of their wedding date, my grandparents, as self-described young, green country kids, were joined in wedlock on Christmas Day, 1917. Thereafter, my grandfather was duly ribbed for being so tight he didn't give my grandmother both a wedding gift and a Christmas gift. Truth be known, he was probably straining his meager finances to pay for the marriage license, rings, and preacher.

Regardless, their marriage endured for sixty-three years. At a family gathering when their life together was well past its half-century mark, my aunt asked my grandfather how their marriage had lasted so long. His answer was short and simple: "By fightin' and scratchin.'" As with many of his observations, the few words he spoke were the tip of the proverbial iceberg, barely betraying much that remained unsaid.

It may come as no great surprise to those with some experience in life that mysteriously, very divergent personalities sometimes bond with a strength of heart and mind that stands as a monument to love and devotion. As every husband and wife must confront the inevitable irritations and annoyances of life such as an overcharge on a bill or a supposedly repaired automobile that just didn't run the way it was supposed to, so it was with my grandparents. On more than one occasion, such instances would prompt an oft repeated scene in their rather spacious country kitchen. Having laid the day's activities to rest and eaten a simple evening meal, the quietness of the night would yield to a serious discussion as to what course of action should be taken concerning a particular problem. With my grandfather comfortably settled in his rocking chair, newspaper in hand, my grandmother would rattle the windows with her impressive command of the King's English (and probably more than a few highly descriptive phrases that would have made any self-respecting king blush). My grandfather would slowly rock and turn the pages of his newspaper while for twenty minutes or so, my grandmother would clearly articulate her doubts and concerns regarding the legitimacy, moral fiber, intelligence, and sanity of the person responsible for the problem at hand. After airing her opinions, she would pause, look at my grandfather, and ask, "Well, Claude, what do you think?"

As his newspaper slowly fell into his lap, he would look at her and respond, "Now, Martha, this is what we're going to do." Seldom did his response bear any more than a pale resemblance to anything my grandmother had said. Though one may wonder if he would not have expressed the same assessment of a situation had she said nothing, their love and respect for one another gave each the right to state their mind and my grandmother was not bashful about doing so. But when my grandfather spoke, a decision had been reached.

It is a pity that my grandparents never ran for public office. In keeping with the great American legend surrounding the humble origins of folks like Abraham Lincoln, both were born in log cabins. These simple structures were the homes available to them. In the context of their times, such homes were neither quaint nor historic; they were merely representative of the area's standard of living and bore little or no difference from those of their neighbors.

Their home was located in the northern portion of Coffee County, a few hundred feet southeast of a small stream called Kelsey Branch which was near a wide spot in the stream called Ivy Lake and long used as the local "swimmin' hole." The cabin in which my grandfather was born was a single story building structure of hewn half-dovetailed beams. Its gable roof was oriented in line with the long axis of the structure. I don't recall a chimney. The cabin may originally have been heated by means of a cast iron stove connected to a ceiling mounted flue. My grandfather's cabin measured about ten by twenty feet. It was built in the nineteenth century and likely used by numerous tenants, hired hands, and local families over the course of many years before finally becoming uninhabitable. In common with those who had once called it home, it could not hide its years.

By comparison, the Coffee County log cabin in which my grandmother was born was almost palatial. Built in the 1880s on family property southwest of the crossroads community of Shady Grove and near the right bank of appropriately named Mud Creek, this sturdy structure was fashioned from hewn half-dovetail notched beams. It stood a story and a half high, sported a substantial sandstone block chimney, and measured about fifteen by twenty feet. It was similar to comparable structures found in Appalachia, southern Illinois, the Ozarks, and eastern Texas. Though a combined frame kitchen and dining area was added in later years, this farmhouse was to serve as home for my great-grandparents and their thirteen children. Still in family hands, the cabin has entered its second century of service.

As newlyweds in 1918, my grandparents proudly moved into the first home they might call their own. Previously used to house tenants on an area farm, their humble structure was recalled many years later as "a ten by twenty foot shack." Small though it may have been, it was more than sufficient to hold their meager worldly possessions and to serve as their home for their first two years of marriage.

Shortly before making their decision to move to Nashville, the wood shingle roof of the small shack caught fire one day while my grandfather was teaching school. My grandmother who was several months pregnant with my Aunt Inez, was forced to quickly pump several buckets of water, grab a ladder and climb atop the burning roof to extinguish the flaming shingles. Though they did not recall their first home in later years with much nostalgia, neither did they exhibit much sympathy for modern newlyweds who whined about the smallness of their apartments which were equipped with running water, electricity, and flush toilets.

In common with a sizable portion of the post-World War I rural population, my grandparents joined the flood of hill country immigrants in the early 1920s who made their way to Nashville in search of economic opportunity. Placed in the context of their rural upbringings, the "big city" was a place of wonderment filled with fancy stores, regular paychecks, and streets teeming with busy people in search of a more promising future. Among the many interesting people my grandmother met shortly after her arrival was a spunky—single, thank you, and destined to remain that way—urbane young lady who was also out to make her way in the world. These two women, my very down-to-earth grandmother and this polished-independent-minded city girl, developed a bond so deep and lasting that they came to see one another as sisters. Coming from a family of eleven children, my grandmother's heart could always accommodate a new member. Her lifelong friend, Beatrice Womack, became simply "Aunt Bea" to an ever increasing number of new-found nieces and nephews. The bond between these sisters was so great that in death half a century later, they came to rest side by side in the rural calm of Coffee County.

Early on in their joint explorations of Nashville, Aunt Bea managed to talk my grandmother into attending an authentic operatic performance which was being presented in Ryman Auditorium. Her descriptions of the musical and lyrical beauty awaiting them overcame my grandmother's lack of enthusiasm and the two ladies soon found themselves seated in the darkened theater beholding the performance. It didn't take long for my grandmother to come to the realization that this kind of fancy music was not her kind of music. Valiantly she stayed put in her seat whether it was out of concern for her friend's feelings or simply to see if things got any better. Finally, she excused herself during the Intermission to brazenly enjoy a cigarette in the lobby. The Intermission ended. The performance continued. My grandmother was still in the lobby doing her best to smoke through a pack of Lucky Strikes, one puff at a time.

When the opera ended, Aunt Bea found her in the lobby. After gushing on about how much she had enjoyed the grand performance, she said to my grandmother, "Oh, Mrs. Mac, you missed the best part. Why didn't you come back in for the rest of the opera?"

With more honesty than was probably called for, my grandmother promptly responded, "I've been listening to fat women with big titties bellowing at the top of their lungs all my life and I ain't going to pay for the privilege!"

It is a fact that in the remaining fifty-five years of her life, my grandmother never again attended an opera. Her candor and lively sense of humor were on full display when she recounted one of her favorite stories about a young mother and her ailing baby.

According to my grandmother, there was a young, green-assed country girl who was doing good to know where babies came from much less what to do with them. Her baby took sick and cried and screamed for days on end. After doing everything she could think of—which wasn't much—she sent a neighbor's son to fetch the local doctor.

When the elderly doctor arrived, he began to look, poke, prod and feel the crying baby.

By this time, the young mother was becoming frantic with worry. "Oh, doctor," she asked. "What can we do?"

Not one to be easily ruffled, the old doctor peered over his spectacles and asked the young woman if she had any tallow in the house.

"Oh, yes," she cried.

"Good," he replied. "Get it, take it into the kitchen, melt a good dab of it in the frying pan, and then rub it all over the baby's backside."

Somewhat surprised, the young mother asked, "Doctor, will that help?"

Still peering over his glasses, the old doctor calmly replied, "Well, I don't know—but it damned sure can't hurt."

While exploring the byways of Middle Tennessee in the late 1960s, I noticed a sign just a few miles shy of the Rutherford-Cannon county line which brought to the attention of passing motorists that "Uncle" Dave Macon was laid to rest in the Coleman Cemetery adjacent to the highway. Students and devotees of country music will readily recall that this talented banjo player was one of the early "'tars" of the infant country music industry and long a mainstay of the pioneer instrumental-only music days of the Grand Old Opry, broadcast to countless farm families since 1925 on station WSM in Nashville.

In the course of visiting my grandfather shortly thereafter, I remarked upon seeing the grave of this country music notable. He recalled having heard this gentleman play at square dances and country gatherings in his youth in the hill country of Cannon County. With something of a grunt, he wryly observed, "I knew him when he was just plain Dave Macon."

It seems that no matter how old we get, there is something special about birthdays. For some, it is an opportunity to celebrate with good friends; for others, it is a quiet time spent with one's family. So it was in the 1970s with my grandmother well into her eighth decade when another candle was placed on top of a crowded cake.

My mother and her sister, Aunt Inez, joined forces and culinary talents to prepare a good home-cooked meal with all the trimmings and do all they could to pamper "Mama." Following an enjoyable afternoon meal, my mother and aunt began casting about to find some way for the three of them to indulge in an all too rare unrushed drive through the countryside.

After some deliberation, the conversation took a drift toward "old-timey" things such as pie safes, butter churns, and sad irons. The two sisters suggested a trip from Manchester, my grandmother's home, to nearby McMinnville to visit a well-stocked antique store. My grandmother was not overly enthusiastic about the idea.

"Oh, Mama," my aunt said, "You would enjoy looking at all the interesting antiques. Doesn't that sound like fun?'"

With a snort of disdain, my grandmother responded, "I grew up with that old shit and I don't care if I ever see that stuff again!"

Doing something as simple as going shopping with my grandmother on the courthouse square in the heart of Manchester was akin to attending a short seminar on family history. It never failed that while going from shop to shop we always ran into yet another relative whom I had never met. Regardless of how distant the relationship, she knew them all. The descendants of ancestors three and four generations removed were readily identified by known relationship and a rapid recounting by name of every generation and likely all of the children in each family.

During the course of numerous family reunions and gatherings, I recall older family members convening over the kitchen table, enjoying their cups of coffee and engaging in discussions of family history which might last for several hours. Names, dates of marriages, births, and deaths, places of birth and burial, and personal details relating to the lives and times of the various relatives were discussed and recounted in detail. No skeleton in the family closet was buried deep enough for them not to uncover and elaborate on. This process of discussing and increasing their knowledge of family history was an ingrained, indelible part of their values and upbringing. Their deep roots in the area extended back for generations. Family was important and knowledge of its members provided a sense of belonging and purpose which is all too often, lost in the rush of our contemporary life.

Although as a young man my grandfather believed his drive and ambition would take him far in life, his ultimate choice of livelihood likely surpassed his wildest expectations. Shortly after moving to Nashville in the early 1920s, he secured a position with the US Post Office. For the next 35 years he worked for the Rail Postal Service out of the now closed Union Station terminal in downtown Nashville. During the course of his career with the

"R.P.O.," he literally traveled hundreds of thousands of miles across the land.

As a child, I enjoyed playing a game with him which I secretly called "Name a Town." The rules were simple: I would browse a road map from an adjacent state, carefully search for some small town in a remote area, and then ask my grandfather if he knew where it was located. Invariably, he would know where it was, how large it was, and the principal businesses located there and of course, if it had a post office. Only when I chanced upon the rare community that did not have a post office which were few and far between, was it possible for me to stump him. His yardstick for measuring the size of a town had nothing to do with census figures, but rather was based on how large a bag of mail was retrieved on the mail car's bag hook as they passed through a town. When I once asked him about all of the interesting places he had been and seen, he grumbled, "I never got a chance to see them—we were too busy sorting the mail."

Folks in those days were a pragmatic and hardworking lot who also possessed a matter-of-fact and often understated sense of humor like the time my Uncle Fred and Aunt Gertrude were driving me and my cousin, Doyle, to Nashville. The long and short of it was that Doyle was thirsty and he continued to pester his parents about his need for a drink of water. Finally, Uncle Fred pulled off the highway and stopped next to a small stream. My cousin jumped out of the car and ran toward the creek to take a drink. Suddenly, he stopped dead in his tracks when he realized that the stream wasn't spring-fed, but just a muddy creek full of dead bugs and such. Upon hearing his concerns, my aunt calmly offered him some sage advice: "Oh, Honey, don't worry about that. It's already been drunk and pissed in a half dozen times."

The fact that Southerners have long established preferences in food will come as no surprise. Taste tempting regional delights like fried chicken, country ham, okra, black-eyed peas, turnip greens, hominy grits, and especially cornbread come to mind. Good cornbread is sweet, creamy, and melts in your mouth. Served hot with a big dab of country butter, it has accented many a delightful meal. With one notable exception, my grandmother was a truly wonderful lady and I loved her dearly. Her many outstanding attributes such as compassion, honesty, and dedication to her family have done much to influence my life. But truth be known, she was not a good cook. Though the specifics remain one of life's unsolved mysteries, she managed over a period of years to perfect the recipe for what could easily rank as the "South's Worst Cornbread." It did not gracefully crumble, rather it shattered. It did not melt in one's mouth, but lay there on the plate, daring you to try and chew it. Each bite had the crackle and constitution of fine-grit sandpaper and replied with a vengeance on its journey to gastronomic oblivion. As a result, I may be the only Southerner that never developed a true appreciation for this delightful dish because of my grandmother's cooking skills.

Based upon informal conversations through the years with a good many folks in the countryside, I have long suspected that a much unappreciated aspect of their traditional values was heavily influenced by the politics and patriotic fervor associated with a time before their great-grandparents were infants. Many of the country folk throughout the region hold folks with aristocratic airs and pretentions at arm's length along with a healthy dose of suspicion and skepticism. Indeed, the mere mention of royalty and noble titles will at the least elicit a serious lack of interest and will prompt some to say things like "We don't have any use for those kind of people" or "Titles are nothing but foolishness." In the end, they hold true to hard work, personal responsibility and common decency. Many of the people who were born, lived and died in my part of the South were plain-spoken, yet could be generous to a fault. They may have had little in the way of financial wealth, but they had big hearts and loved their families. And they knew how to cook as I can attest to from many a meal. I enjoyed it all—except my grandmother's cornbread.

12

A Country Teacher

DONALD BALL

FOLLOWING IN THE FOOTSTEPS OF MY NO-NONSENSE GRANDFA-
ther a half-century earlier, I, too, attended Middle Tennessee State
University (MTSU) and emerged in January 1970 from that fine
institution with a brand new hot-off-the-press bachelor's degree in
history. I was prepared to make the great transition from student
to teacher over half a century after my grandfather had made the
same journey. And a rapid transition it was, having literally graduated on one Sunday evening and being required to report to my
teaching assignment the following day.

Bright and early the next morning I was walking the halls
of Flintville High School and was soon ready to greet for the
first time my students in American History, sophomore English,
and the lone study hall with which I was charged. Named for the
small crossroads settlement in which it is located, Flintville High
School is situated in the southeastern portion of Lincoln County,
Tennessee, just a few miles north of the Tennessee-Alabama state
line. Resting along the break from the gentle rolling hills of the

expansive Central Basin, it merged into the rugged, heavily dissected slopes of the Cumberland Plateau. The economy of the area is primarily agricultural and, not surprisingly, many of the students in my classes were the children of hard working farm families.

Though they may have been a little rough around the edges when it came to naming all of the presidents or giving a polished book report in front of their fellow classmates, they knew the surrounding countryside like the back of their hand. I came to learn much about the area from my conversations with them. To this day, my experiences as a teacher prompt me to rate that period of my life as the most personally rewarding position I have ever held. It was a privilege to have met and interacted with so many warm and hospitable families in the life of this rural community.

Having a long-standing interest in all things archaeological, I made sure that each class became acquainted with the prehistory of the region. I was soon swamped with invitations from various students to visit their respective farms, meet their parents, and walk the fields looking for "Indian heads" (arrowheads) and other items. In some cases, conversations with the family would lead to suggestions that I might also visit this cousin or that uncle. On more than one occasion I would find myself heading off to yet a second farm and making additional acquaintances in the area.

Weather and other obligations like grading papers and preparing for class aside, these trips afforded me a rare chance to come to know at least some of my students at both school and home. In visiting with parents on an informal one-to-one basis, it became possible to work out some of their children's student-related problems in a totally relaxed manner at a very grass roots level. Working with parents to encourage their children to read, or help a child with their homework, or just checking to see that homework had in fact been done were all basic matters that could best be handled on the home front. With the help of their parents, the results were often better grades on report cards. Of course, family situations varied widely and some domestic circumstances were such that educational advancement for some students was a very difficult if not impossible task. Over time, I came to understand that not every problem can be resolved with a textbook solution. There are times when a little creativity goes a long way and one begins to realize that some professors spent the first half of a course telling you about teaching and the second half trying to prompt you to confront problems not discussed in the first half. My experiences with two students in particular illustrate the truth of the contrast between textbook and real-life teaching.

Though I have altered the names of the students, the following events which transpired during an otherwise quiet period near the end of the school year, have long remained fresh in my mind. Among the many students with whom I frequently interacted, Jay and Matt often accompanied me on various afternoon visits to area farms to look for arrowheads and truth be known, get in a little extra gum-flapping time with a buddy or two from school in the process.

The two young men came from very different backgrounds. In the case of Jay, his father was a no-nonsense gentleman retired after many years of honorable military service. He was a man who gave serious thought to the education and career paths both Jay and his younger brother might take, guiding both toward college and government service. Jay had been raised in an orderly, nurturing environment which placed heavy emphasis on school work and it clearly showed.

Matt was not so fortunate. His parents were poorly educated tenant farmers barely able to make ends meet in the process of raising several children. From comments made by both Matt and several other students, I learned that it was not uncommon for Pa to spend any available money on liquor. He would often return home drunk, raising hell with the family for much of the night. On one occasion, Pa began beating on his family and Ma was forced to defend both herself and the children by holding her husband at bay with a large butcher knife until he at last passed out—hardly a home environment conducive for nurturing young minds.

With the end of the school year drawing near, I made a point to purchase two Canadian silver dollars at one of the many flea markets in the region. On one of our last outings I presented a silver dollar to each boy as a memento of our travels and as a way of thanking them for their enjoyable companionship. Jay quietly accepted the coin, gave it a brief glance, and offered an appropriate and polite "Thank you." Matt, on the other hand, was beside himself. His eyes grew wide and a bright smile beamed from his face. I thought for a moment that the young man was going to pee in his britches while thanking me. The truth of the event seemed apparent. Throughout his entire school experience, no teacher may have ever bestowed upon him any significant act of kindness or generosity. To many teachers, he might have been just another poor, unmotivated student with few or no prospects. To me, he was one of the many special people I was privileged to meet and learn from as a teacher.

As much as we might wish to make a difference, it is not possible for a teacher to inspire every student. Though some personalities and situations cannot be overcome despite our best efforts, some often small but nonetheless notable successes serve to make our efforts worth it. I have commented on Matt and the trying home situation he faced on an almost daily basis. Things were not easy for the young man and that's putting it mildly. Academically, his grades may only be termed as consistently poor. When I took over as a mid-year replacement for a teacher on maternity leave, I promptly reviewed appropriate grade book entries for my classes. Matt, a sophomore English student, had received three D's in a row for the preceding grading periods and not surprisingly, a D for the previous semester.

During the course of my semester with him things began to change—slowly at first and then more rapidly. Matt was one of the first and certainly one of the more enthusiastic field-walkers to accompany me on my afternoon excursions. As the semester progressed, his grade for the first six-weeks was his customary D. The following grading periods began to show improvement, first a C and then a B. No brownie or extra-credit points were promised or given. Every increase was both earned and deserved. Matt did it on his own in response to a teacher treating him with kindness and respect.

As the term progressed, the normally quiet Matt also became more active in classroom discussions. He not only did his required assignments, but began asking about extra-credit books reviews and other projects, and seemed to come alive in his interactions with other students. The basic truth of the matter was not difficult to see. His self-esteem and confidence had taken a giant leap forward. No longer was he just another kid burdened with homework, he was now in the position to teach the teacher about the subject he knew best—the open countryside with its farms and fields and places of interest that only a son of the land would know. When the conclusion of the school year arrived, Matt received a C for the semester and a C- for the year, the highest grade he had ever received for any class. Though a small triumph in the annals of education, it was possible to bring out some small portion of the potential which had lain dormant within him for far too long.

In a day and age increasingly saturated with the marvels of modern telecommunications technology, we seem to exhibit an almost boundless glee entertaining ourselves with the latest techno-toy which will perform yet another mindless task in the blink of an eye. Unlike an older generation which received its news long after the fact, we are now able to worry about things instantly thanks to the Internet, cellular telephones, and cable news networks. My experience indicates that these modern miracles of communication are only slightly faster and infinitely more expensive than the "student grapevine." Though some physicists may disagree, I believe a good case may be built that the fastest thing known to humankind is not the speed of light, but rather bad news and hot gossip.

For example, nearing dusk and winding up another of my frequent after-school visits to farms in the area, I was driving down one of Lincoln County's many pastoral roads accompanied by two of the young men from one of my classes. I glimpsed the sight of a young girl sitting on the bank of a small stock pond close to the road. The simple fact of someone enjoying a quiet, reflective moment was not what caught my eye, but rather it was the worried and distraught look emanating from the young lady's face.

Glancing to one of the boys riding with me, I commented, "She looks familiar, but I don't recall her name. Doesn't she go to Flintville High School?"

One of the young men promptly responded, "Oh, yeah, that's Betty Lou Smith; she got knocked up by Joe Daniels and ain't worked up the nerve to tell her Pa yet."

As much as forbidden fruit is always sweeter, so it is that a whispered conversation with one's friends during class. I myself have participated in many a long and delightful conversation with lots of folks throughout the years. I would never want to be viewed as opposed to a good old-fashion bull session, except when I am teaching a class. I had a very possessive attitude concerning being the captain of that craft of knowledge and was not particularly inclined to yield the helm to the crew.

Despite knowing better, some of the bolder sophomore boys remained persistent in yielding to temptation. Forms of discipline like beheading and bullwhips came to mind, but seemed a bit harsh. Still, it remained necessary to maintain order using methods which were both humane and effective in dealing with wagging tongues and raging hormones. Experimentation over a period of several weeks yielded a useful insight into how to deal with the problem. Verbal warnings alone, especially several to the same person, seemed to represent a youthful example of "standing up to authority" and engendering respect among one's peers. A desire to impress one's friends far outweighed irritating the teacher. But a teenage audience can be very fickle in how it views such teacher/student interactions. It finally dawned on me that the solution to the problem rested not in me being the lone custodian of discipline, but rather in marshaling the assistance of a majority of class members in a manner which would discourage, not encourage, impromptu adolescent chit-chat.

I tried a new approach which surpassed my wildest expectations and also served to provide some theatrical relief to an increasingly tiresome situation. This small production called for but one prop, a large, heavy oak desk placed center stage before the audience, and demanded little rehearsal on the part of the actors.

Within days, the script to this production had been memorized by each student. This short one-act play—with no spoken parts—was titled "The Dying Cockroach." It became an instant hit.

The plot of this human drama was the essence of simplicity and quickly became the "Standard Operating Procedure" for young gentlemen caught talking (young ladies were exempt for obvious reasons). A stern look, a point of the finger, and the words "Dying Cockroach," resulted with the young man in question "assuming the position." And what a position it was. Backing up to the short axis of the sturdy oak desk thoughtfully provided by the Lincoln County Board of Education, the talkative lad would lean back on the top of the desk and raise both arms and legs skyward. I would continue with the class while the limbs of the "cockroach" began to sway and wobble after several minutes. During this time, various classmates would inevitably pop off with giggles or comments on how silly the individual looked. After a short period of amusing, rather than impressing, their peers, tongues were not as inclined to waggle during class.

Even normally active, bright-eyed young scholars seem to give into the "dreaded drowsies" after lunch on a sunny spring afternoon. Despite my best efforts to keep the pace of learning lively and interesting, it was easy to spot heavy eyelids slowly sinking into the sunset. Though setting a fuse to a keg of gunpowder outside the window would doubtless have perked them up, I suspected that the School Board might not approve.

In the process of casting about for a more subdued, humane way to regain the attention of my drifting students, it struck me that the School Board in its infinite, all-knowing wisdom had already supplied the necessary tools. Then as now, many text books tend to be rather substantial tomes. As eyelids fluttered, I would slowly amble toward the heavy oak desk in the front center of the classroom while continuing to talk about the subject at hand and casually pick up the text lying there. Then I would proceed to slam the broad face of the book down on the top of the desk. The resulting thunderclap would shake the walls and rattle the old structure's windows. Eyelids would fly open, heads would snap up, and without missing a beat the lecture continued with, "As I was saying . . ."

During the middle of my semester at Flintville, an unexpected death in my immediate family necessitated my being out of state for several school days on short notice. In my absence, arrangements were made for a local lay preacher to serve as a substitute teacher. Although the majority of the following week was extremely hectic, I had little doubt that my young scholars would enjoy a brief vacation from that strange teacher who did unusual things like give homework assignments and actually expected them to be done. Who was also known to do unexpected things such as beat on a trash can or slam the room's heavy door shut to bring them back to earth after lunch-time.

I was surprised and a bit shocked when not one, but several students approached me upon my return and remarked, "Oh, Mr. Ball, we're so glad you're back! Let me tell you about the substitute teacher." It seems in life that there are always trade-offs. Where my classroom presentations were kept as lively as the law and the school board would allow, my replacement was perceived as boring and dull. Where I was viewed as demanding but fair, he was seen as dictatorial. Through the years, I have come to view this experience as exemplifying the old adage, "Better the devil you know than one you don't."

With the school year winding down, I gave much thought as to how best to utilize our remaining class time for the benefit of my students. Particularly in the case of my sophomore English classes, I was confronted with the reality that due to a number of personal reasons often related to family financial considerations, some of my young scholars would be quitting school and seeking permanent employment. With all due respect to the great authors, I was hard pressed to see that further study of either iambic pentameter poetry or turgid prose would serve my students better than an intensive reexamination of certain front-of-the-book basic nuts and bolts areas like rules of grammar and rudimentary communications skills. Our review of what seemed to me to be a basic, useful skill in life—the preparation of a business letter—quickly convinced me of the wisdom of devoting time to these topics.

Though I have kept no student samples through the years, the general no-frills, grab the bull-by-the-horns, frontal-assault style displayed by many of the class exercises went something on the order of:

DEAR Sir plesesendme yourNew catalogg encloseis monneyorder for 3dollarsend to George Green route6 box 27 flintville Tennessee real fast thankyousincerely

george Green

To give credit where credit is due, several major business points such as who, what, how much, etcetera were addressed. Then again, these diamonds were a bit rough around the edges. To this day, I remain of the opinion that the effort spent honing such real-world skills was time well spent in attempting to let their last days of school be of real, practical use to my students.

As we are often told, all good things must come to an end. Shortly before the end of the school term I received a "Greetings" letter from Uncle Sam and soon thereafter found myself being treated to an "all-expenses-paid" trip to boot camp and subsequent military service in Berlin, Germany. Following that phase of my life, I opted to take advantage of the G. I Bill and pursue graduate level education in anthropology at the University of Tennessee. As events subsequently unfolded in my life I never again sought employment as a teacher, but despite the passage of now of half a century, I have often reflected upon my time spent in trying to educate the young scholars in Flintville High School. It has remained my hope that some small vestige of my efforts has remained alive and well in the minds of my former students as has their time with me graced my memory.

13

Sweet Tea Serenade

MICHAEL BRASWELL

HATTIE FREEMAN, MY GRANDMOTHER, WAS BORN IN THE LATE 1800s. She was the kind of woman you wanted on the wagon train with you headed west just in case you came under attack. Barely five feet tall, she wore her two braided pig tails wrapped and pinned around her head during the day and let them fall to her sides at night before bedtime, making her look like an old Indian woman. Twenty-five years younger than her husband, Uriah "Ken" Kindred, she bore ten children—eight boys and two girls—with one of her sons dying of a fever before he was ten. When they lost their farm in the Great Depression, she worked the fields alongside her husband and children as sharecroppers and tenant farmers. It was a hard life, but Hattie was a tough woman. She cooked, cleaned, ploughed and prayed. And she made her and her daughter's dresses from calico feed sacks. When her jaw set and her eyes turned steel blue, someone was about to catch hell. Like the time she told her husband, Ken, if he ever whipped another one of their boys with a razor strap, she would shoot him. When his memory lapsed and he ordered the oldest to go fetch the strap and prepare for a whipping, Hattie simply called out his name, "Ken," and pointed to the mantle over the fireplace where she kept the Colt 32 her father had given her. Her husband cleared his throat and ordered his relieved son to go split some firewood. That was then, long before I knew her.

My extended visits to the unpainted farmhouse on a country dirt road where my Grandmama, as we called her, lived started in the mid-1950s. Of course, family visits started long before then. I always got my father to stop at a country store so I could buy her a can of Buttercup or Peach Blossom snuff, her two favorites. She and my Aunt Sara lived together. My aunt taught elementary school in another town, leaving my grandmama to her chickens, milk cow and garden during the day. Aunt Sara never married. The family rumor mill attributed it to a failed romance during World War II although later in life she did turn down a marriage proposal from the town mayor, who was something of a blowhard and ladies' man. Who knows why she never married? Maybe she saw enough of her brothers over the years and the men she did date to decide staying with her mother was a safer choice. In any event, her extended summer vacations, cruises and long weekends in the town where she taught meant that I, being the oldest grandson, was elected to companion duty with Grandmama. It proved to be more of a pleasure than a duty. Even as a middle-aged man long after my grandmama had passed, when I once hugged an elderly woman who smelled of dried sweat and snuff, I couldn't help but smile as childhood memories flooded back.

Each morning in the old farmhouse began with hoecake, a skillet-sized biscuit amply spread with country butter. Thick slices of cured bacon with a rind and cane syrup for the sopping up chunks of biscuit completed the meal. When figs were in season, cane syrup was often supplanted by preserves and jams made from whole figs, cooked and simmered in their own juices. Coffee laced with milk and sugar was the beverage of choice. Then came feeding the chickens and gathering their eggs which was a task I readily embraced while she milked Guernsy, her lone milk cow.

From chickens and the milk cow, Hattie moved to her garden until lunchtime while I made up imaginary baseball and war games or explored the nearby woods. Cooked turnip, collard, or mustard greens seasoned with a chunk of ham hock, and skillet fried corn bread were on the menu for dinner along with oven-baked sweet potatoes and sweet tea to drink. That's where the good news ends. Supper was another matter. Breakfast, check. Dinner, check. Supper, survived. If you have never tried to eat cold turnip greens, you have little reason to complain about whatever you are served. While cold sweet potatoes are edible, cold greens and cornbread will dampen the heartiest of appetites. That said, I was always fascinated by two things regarding food that my Grandmama preferred. One was the way she would delicately peel a sweet potato and slowly relish each bite as if it was the finest dessert available on earth. Her second rule was that she would never eat chicken—even fried chicken! When I asked her why, she replied that she had wrung so many chicken necks raising her family that she no longer had a taste for chicken of any kind.

Family reunions were another sight to behold, less like "The Waltons" and more like "Christmas Vacation." Covered dishes layered the long dining room table while casseroles and other fixings kept the country kitchen abuzz with female chatter. The men told tall tales and argued about who had the best car, truck or riding lawn mower in the living room while the women sized each other up and jockeyed for a higher pecking order rank in the kitchen and dining room. Meanwhile, us cousins ran wild in the dusty yard, mimicking our parents as children often do. I still remember my uncle Jimmy's response when I introduced him to my fiancée. When he asked her what kind of car she was driving, she responded that it was a Pontiac Firebird. He grunted and said, "I'll bet my Buick Electra 225 will outrun it."

When the reunion was over and the two of us were back into our rocking chairs, sipping sweet tea well into the night, Hattie would provide me with a commentary complete with footnotes concerning the day's happenings. Some daughters-in-law she liked, some she didn't. Floramarene, who at almost six feet tall and two hundred plus pounds, always looked to me like she could have been a Marine, was not one of my grandmama's favorites. Her attempts at sweetness were awkward and poorly practiced while scowling at her husband when she thought no one was looking, came quickly and easily. When talking about her, Grandmama's reference was typically "hussy" or "heifer." Then there was also Henrrieta who at barely five feet tall, weighed the same as Floramarene. She frequently attributed her weight to "gland" problems, causing Hattie's eyes to narrow and mutter, "It's not a gland problem. It's a hand problem."

During my growing up years through the age of thirteen, my grandmama's affection probably kept me from becoming a juvenile delinquent. Every time my father brought me out to stay with her, I could see it in her eyes and subtle smile—she was glad to see me. While things weren't always going smoothly at home, I often felt more at home with her. I could trust this woman born in the 1800s with any question I had and she always seemed to have an answer that satisfied my queries. During those years, she was my best friend and our favorite time of the day was after supper.

Porch time. End of the day time. Sipping strong, sweet tea, rocking in our chairs, talking and listening—mostly listening to the life she shared with her young grandson was the best of times. Hattie talked about her horse and buggy growing up years, how her two uncles both fought in the Civil War, in the Battle of Gettysburg, and survived to ride their horse, Legion, back home to their farm in Georgia. And how they rode all the way back to that same battlefield for the first North and South Veterans' reunion. She also reveled in telling me stories about spirits and ghosts as I listened in wide-eyed wonder. According to her, because she was born with a caul over her face, she had the gift of "second sight." She looked at me with a patient seriousness and said, "Spirits don't visit you to cause you harm. They come to tell you something about yourself or your future that you need to know. The only folks who get hurt are the ones who do something foolish out of fear." Once she told me a story about some kind of large animal that ran under her house and raised it off its foundation. Her father shot at it, but all they found was a bit of bloody fur, a kind they had never seen before, hanging on a stretch of barbed wire fence. Sometimes when she was on a ghost story roll, I would turn my back to the open windows and stare at the wall until I went to sleep, afraid that the fireflies fluttering about outside might be some kind of spirit's eyes. Hattie possessed a great sense of wonder and curiosity in both the natural and spirit worlds. She taught herself to read with her children's books by the light from the fireplace. As the years passed, I realized much of my own imagination and sense of wonder came from her tutelage.

Trying to raise nine children during the Great Depression is something my generation knew nothing about. Going to town to buy your children much needed shoes for school, but coming back with only a pair of socks for each of them because that's all you could afford. Not having the money to pay or anything else to barter for the country doctor to come visit a seriously ill or injured child, hardened her will to survive. Since they sold all their eggs for essentials, my father once told me that for him and his siblings' birthdays, they got an egg cooked any way they liked. And then, there was the time their father was away working at a saw mill when a drunk tried to break into the house. Hattie apparently had all her children sit against the far wall while she retrieved her trusty Colt 32 and hollered at the inebriated man, "Come on in. I have something for you." When halfway through the window, he saw her aiming her pistol at him, he broke and ran. That's when Hattie ran out on the front porch and emptied the revolver in his direction, apparently wounding him, but not bad enough to keep him from stumbling toward the cover of the woods.

My grandmama sent three sons off to fight in Europe during World War II. All of them survived the war, but one barely. Uncle Dorsey was shot twice by a German sniper in France during the battle for St Lo. Twice the surgeons gave him up for dead only to find him still alive on the gurney they had rolled into the hospital hallway. She never quite forgave President Roosevelt for taking her sons to war.

Once when I was nine years, she made it abundantly clear during one of our evening porch sitting sessions that she had no use for the white trash that lived a quarter of a mile down the road. Furthermore, if they tried to steal her chickens again, she planned to fill them as she put it, "with hot lead." The fact that she had extra locks for the two doors accessing the bedroom where we slept, one leading to the living room and the other to the front porch, illustrated her concern for our safety. More evidence to that effect was the Colt 32 she kept under her pillow and the axe and automatic 22 rifle that were located next to her bed. She was ready not only to protect what was hers, but also go after those who might choose to threaten her or her possessions. Deep into the second night I was roused by her from my sleep. "Grab hold of the back of my nightgown," she whispered. It was pitch black, but I held on for dear life as Hattie, armed with her rifle pulled me along. As we moved quietly toward the back door, I could her the chickens cackling nervously. When we arrived at the back door, she instructed me to let go of her nightgown. She kicked the screen open and stepping out on the back steps, hollered, "Take this, you sons of bitches" as she fired off ten rounds in a long arc around the large cedar tree where the chickens roosted each night. I stood petrified as I listened to whoever it was trying to steal her chickens, crash through bushes and briars as they ran for their lives. Like I said previously, if you were ever under attack, you wanted Hattie, armed and dangerous, in your company.

Like all things, what time brings us, time also takes away. When Hattie was sixty-eight, she had a stroke. She had been diagnosed with an enlarged heart years earlier which is why as she told me, the doctor told her to drink a glass of concord grape Mogen David wine each evening. Perhaps, that was his prescription and maybe as she interpreted it, a larger glass of wine increased her chances for good health. While the stroke left her frail, she still had her keen wit and strong will. Another result was that her blue eyes seemed brighter and more luminous than ever before.

I went off to college and she and Aunt Sara continued on at the farmhouse. I called her most weeks with a joke I thought she would like and when I came home, I brought her a chocolate milk-shake, her favorite, to enjoy as we reminisced about old times. After I got married, the calls continued. I still remember the last call I made to her. It wasn't on Saturday when I usually talked to her, but for some reason, I felt the urge and acted on it. The joke was a good one and we had a great laugh together. Thirty minutes later, at eighty-three years of age, Grandmama had another stroke and went into a coma. It would be the last joke I would tell her, the last time I would talk to her. I have always wished I could remember the joke. It was a good one. When my father read her will, he was instructed to take a pillowcase from the place she had hidden it and sewn the ends together. Opening it, he found twelve hundred one dollar bills she had saved over a lifetime. Hattie's instructions were to use that money to take care of her funeral expenses. Any of the money that was left was to go to my aunt who had lived with her all those years. That was just like her, paying her way out of this life as she moved on to the next.

Although time has taken its toll and little is left of the farm or farmhouse, whenever I'm in the area, I still like to ride out to what's left of the old place and sit for a few minutes . . . remembering.

Contributors

Michael Braswell grew up in Moultrie, Georgia, a small town in a primarily farming community. His teaching and writing interests have been in areas related to social justice, peacemaking and the human condition. He has published books on ethics, social justice and human relations as well as two novels and several short story collections.

Anthony Cavender grew up in Nashville, Tennessee. He earned a B.A. in English from Belmont University and a PhD in cultural anthropology from the University of Tennessee. His research focused on ethnomedicine and included stints in Ecuador, Guatemala, Zimbabwe as well as Southern Appalachia. His publications include the books, *Folk Medicine in Southern Appalachia* and *A Tennessee Folklore Sampler*.

Ralph Bland is the author of *Stars Rain Sun Moon*, *Ace*, eight other novels, and two collections of short stories. A native Nashvillian, he lives with his wife and dogs on the outskirts of Music City USA.

Donald Ball is a native of Middle Tennessee whose ancestors first settled in the area around 1820. Don is a retired archaeologist from the U.S. Army Corps of Engineers and resides in Louisville, Kentucky. He has published on not only prehistoric and historic archaeology, but also on a variety of other diverse historical topics.

www.ingramcontent.com/pod-product-compliance
Lightning Source LLC
Chambersburg PA
CBHW071230290326
41931CB00037B/2568